The Thirty-ni: Million Steps

To Derek,

You are the true expert on end-to-ending!

With best wishes and, of course, thoughts of the far North!

Jonathan Richards.

The Thirty-nine Million Steps

Walking the length of a changing nation

JONATHAN RICHARDS

First published 2018

Copyright © Jonathan Richards 2018

The right of Jonathan Richards to be identified
as the author of this work has been asserted in accordance with
the Copyright, Designs & Patents Act 1988.

All rights reserved. No part of this book may be reproduced, stored in a retrieval system, or transmitted in any form or by any means, electronic, electrostatic, magnetic tape, mechanical, photocopying, recording or otherwise, without the written permission of the copyright holder.

Published under licence by Brown Dog Books and
The Self-Publishing Partnership, 7 Green Park Station, Bath BA1 1JB

www.selfpublishingpartnership.co.uk

ISBN printed book: 978-1-78545-249-9
ISBN e-book: 978-1-78545-250-5

Cover design by Kevin Rylands
Internal design by Tim Jollands
All maps and photographs by Jonathan Richards

Printed and bound in the UK

FRONT COVER PICTURE
Footsteps in the sand above Brora, northern Scotland.

*To all those who seek challenges
in their life, and to all those who have
challenges thrust upon them.*

Contents

	Preface	9
	Introduction	11
CHAPTER 1	Land's End – The Tamar Valley	17
CHAPTER 2	The Tamar Valley – The Mendips	29
CHAPTER 3	The Mendips – The Malverns	39
CHAPTER 4	The Malverns – Stafford	54
CHAPTER 5	Stafford – Marple	67
CHAPTER 6	Marple – Huddersfield	76
CHAPTER 7	Huddersfield – Malham	91
CHAPTER 8	Malham – Kirkby Stephen	103
CHAPTER 9	Kirkby Stephen – Hadrian's Wall	116
CHAPTER 10	Hadrian's Wall – Carter Bar	126
CHAPTER 11	Carter Bar – Innerleithen	134
CHAPTER 12	Innerleithen – Edinburgh	145
CHAPTER 13	Edinburgh – Loch Leven	154
CHAPTER 14	Loch Leven – Pitlochry	166
CHAPTER 15	Pitlochry – Carrbridge	180
CHAPTER 16	Carrbridge – The Morangie Forest	190
CHAPTER 17	The Morangie Forest – Golspie	203
CHAPTER 18	Golspie – Lybster	212
CHAPTER 19	Lybster – John o' Groats	221
	The End to End Ballad	230

Preface

Life's path is rarely a continuously flat, even and straightforward passage. More likely, there will be unexpected twists and turns and we may encounter surprise obstacles or, as commuters know, we may be faced with major disruptions and diversions along the way. So it was in this book, which recalls how I set out and walked on my own, without a support team, back-up vehicle or even a mobile phone, from one end of Britain to the other.

I still tell students in my science classes that we are the product of our inherited genes and our environment; I have my parents to thank for many things besides my eye colour and the shape of my nose. My father, whose reputation at cricket for always being 'not out' at the end of a game earned him the nick-name "Red ink Ricardo", taught me never to give up, and my remarkable mother's battle with terminal illness continues to inspire.

None of us can truly look into the future or see what is coming around the bend. When I wrote this account, I couldn't have imagined that my life would have taken the course it has. Decades later, I do find myself in what seems like a different life, in a different world. By walking from Land's End to John o' Groats, I hoped to learn about my native land but also to escape the scramble of modern life. These days, I ride the Beijing metro and may find myself compressed in a sea of humanity, while my state-of-the-art smart-phone even tells me how many steps I really do take each day. But I don't feel enslaved by technology and I don't feel like a sardine packed in Peking style, for I have known freedom, fresh air, independence and adventure and I have found some degree of the fulfillment that I can see people all around me are seeking.

The publication of *The Thirty-Nine Million Steps* itself represents another step along the path to fulfillment. It has been made possible with the expertise and professionalism of Douglas, Heather and their team at SPP, also by the support and understanding of Malika and our boys George and James, who keep me young at heart.

The dedication in this book is really for everyone – all those I have mentioned in this preface, but also for you, dear reader. I hope that you will enjoy and may be inspired, by my story, to take up and meet your own challenges in life. After all, as Einstein might have said, if you throw enough energy at something, anything is possible.

Jonathan Richards, Beijing, 2018

Introduction

Murder forced Richard Hannay, hero of Buchan's *The Thirty-Nine Steps*[1] to make his escape through England and the Scottish Lowlands. There are no murders and no matters of national security in my story, and my escape through Britain was not made from spies, but from the rat race of modern life. Nonetheless, this is an adventure story – in fact, the adventure of a lifetime.

Inspired by such diverse figures as Ian Botham[2] and Jimmy Savile[3], I was thirty-two years old when I first had the notion of taking up Britain's ultimate walking challenge. I began to plan how I could walk, solo, from Land's End to John o' Groats. Why that particular challenge and why not a bungee jump, a cycle ride, a 'Channel swim', or the London Marathon? Well, there were good reasons. Being covered in lard has never appealed, nor did the prospect of dodging car ferries and the like in the world's busiest shipping highway – and I was put off cycling as an undergraduate. From the village of Lympstone on the Exe Estuary I would pedal, painfully, up and down the hills into Exeter, usually laden with weighty tomes such as Grout's 'A History of Western Music', together with my oboe and a cor anglais… and it always rained. When, some years later, I decided to give cycling another go, returning from work one summer evening I passed a lorry outside the Danish bacon depot in Aylesford at precisely the moment

---

[1] *The Thirty-Nine Steps* (1915) by John Buchan is a classic adventure novel. It has been adapted several times for radio, film and TV

[2] Ian Botham is a famous English former sportsman. Best known for his attacking spirit, he inspired many famous victories for England at cricket. He played other sports as well, and raised huge amounts of money for charity when he walked the length of Britain, from north to south.

[3] Jimmy Savile was an entertainer and television comedian. He was one of the first celebrities to become an 'end to ender'.

that animal rights activists detonated the bomb which destroyed it. No, cycling was not for me! I can see the fun in bungee jumping but is anyone really the wiser for a few seconds of terror? The marathon's throng of heaving bodies, a human race through city streets, seemed to sum up the very things I wanted to escape. On the other hand, to experience and understand even a little more about this patchwork land so rich in heritage and so varied in geography, and even fleetingly to pass over and through its hills and forests, its plains and marshes, and to follow its rivers and coastlines, didn't seem so daft after all! So 'End to End' it had to be, and, two years later, one warm day in the second week of July, I was ready to set off.

The planning, as you might imagine, involved quite a bit of research and time spent in the library. I read, or browsed, any number of walking handbooks and guides, as well as stories of those who, like John Hillaby[4], had their own marathon tales to tell. At the same stage in his planning, Hillaby acknowledged that the feat could be done, but wondered whether, at fifty, he could do it. Could I?

Fitness was in my favour. I have a wiry build and teach games as well as science in school. Running and training with the children keep me more or less in shape, and while the physical requirements of carrying a heavy pack for twenty or thirty miles in tough conditions may differ, for example, from the demands of refereeing an under-elevens' football match, barring accident or injury I was always *fairly* confident of making the distance. Stamina would obviously be a factor, but I decided at an early stage that the best strategy would simply be to wait and see if I could keep going, day in, day out – besides which, I am a great believer in the curative powers of sleep. How often do we go to bed 'shattered' and wake up the next day refreshed, renewed and ready for more…? And how else is it that if

---

[4] John Hillaby was a British adventurer and travel writer. His book *Journey Through Britain* (1968) tells the story of his walk from End to End.

INTRODUCTION

you go to bed with the crossword and get stuck with a clue, in the morning the answer is obvious?

But stamina and fitness would not be the only enabling factors. Apart from "Could I?" I had to ask, "Could I fit it in?" and also, as a family man with two young daughters, "Could I get away with it?" In these respects I can count my blessings. For one thing, teaching in the independent sector has its advantages. We work hard and for long hours but the summer break is wonderful! Two clear months is ample time to recharge one's batteries or, I can tell you, to do something useful, like paint the house inside and out, but also enough to walk the length of Britain. I have worked in business, too, and can clearly remember how we used to look forward to the weekend, or to a few days at Christmas, but the school holiday gave me the time I would need. Perhaps there are college students who, like me, appreciate the long holidays but for whom there are other priorities, such as finding employment or repaying debt.

So could I get away with it? It certainly seemed unlikely and, had it not been for the tolerance and support of Lydia, my wife, I am absolutely sure that the project wouldn't have got off the ground at all. Not only did she send me maps and other things along the way, but also she drove all the way from Surrey to meet me in Caithness in a car which, according to one mechanic, following a breakdown, "would never make it." In the meantime, amidst building works at home, she looked after our girls, Isabella, who was six and a half, and Francesca, just three… not to mention battling against floods, an infestation of bugs which swarmed down one of the chimneys, and a direct lightning strike on another! Hers was the real strength during those weeks.

Around one in three of us either have had, or will develop, cancer in some form during our lives, although not necessarily at the end of them. In part, this is due to advances made in medical care and in part due to heightened awareness and screening programmes which assist early diagnosis. It is also due to the work of doctors and scientists committed to understanding the disease. I wanted to help, and chose a high-profile cancer charity for which I would raise sponsor money.

I approached family, friends and local businesses. One idea, which turned out to be very successful, was to set up a three-way liaison between my school, Aberdour, and the local school in the Scottish village from which it took its name. The children sent off letters typically beginning:

"Dear Aberdour School in Scotland,
I am writing to you to tell you about our school…"

… and duly received messages in return. I planned my route to pass through the village and arranged a provisional meeting, if I ever got that far! The journey between Land's End and Aberdour on the coast of Fife would be 680 miles, and the parents at my school were invited to sponsor me for linking the two schools in that leg of my walk. Many generous pledges came in and, by the time I had been photographed with the children, and given interviews for the literary institutions which are *The Banstead Herald* and the *Surrey Mirror*[5] (fame at last?) it was clear that the wheels were well and truly in motion!

There was a lot to do. Naturally, there was the question of gathering together the equipment I would need. A big step was purchasing a large, 'top of the range' rucksack with dozens of features. The instructions were as confusing as those which come with Scandinavian self-assembly furniture, and the writing was minute and in German, leaving me none the wiser. Another key acquisition was my sleeping bag. Compressed into its own bag, it was the same size and weight as a rugby ball. The tent, a two-man 'dome', came from my brother, who had bought it for a holiday which turned from camping into bed and breakfasting after just one soggy and sleepless night. Perhaps, I thought, I would have

---

[5] *The Banstead Herald* and the *Surrey Mirror* are local newspapers with a relatively small circulation.

INTRODUCTION

better luck. The rest of the kit, apart from my camera, a natty Minolta, which was borrowed, came together from 'stock'.

I have about as much hair now as I was born with, according to my mother (at one time I had rather more). Apparently, she would hold me up to the light, to show people that I wasn't a bald baby. My nickname at the cricket club is "Cue Ball" and my friends there responded to my announcement that I would be 'unavailable' for all of our Sunday afternoon fixtures around the villages of Surrey during July and August, by sponsoring me with a new club cap, to be worn at all times. To this, my wife pinned a tiny Mothers' Union badge, in memory of her mother, with whom I had shared a good deal of the preliminary planning. Other important items of clothing included a good fleece and a breathable cagoule. I had two pairs of stout boots, one thoroughly broken in, from long walks in Snowdonia, and the other of the same brand but much newer, to be called into service as and when required.

It may seem, from the description which follows, that the whole affair amounts to something of a glorious 'pub crawl' (Britain's longest, perhaps) and it is true that I crossed the threshold of more than a hundred such establishments in the forty-four days it took me between Cornwall's tip and the cliffs overlooking Orkney and the Pentland Firth! But, for a man in my position, the humble 'boozer' had a lot to offer: shelter, soap and water, soft seats, company, if I wanted it, and food, as well as drink to satisfy my raging thirst, or to take the edge off aches and pains. Many pubs, of course, are the focal point of a community (I couldn't ever find Ambridge or The Bull, but I came to lots of places like it, and one or two "Rovers Returns")[6]

---

[6] The Bull and the Rovers Return are fictional pubs which feature in long-running British soap operas. The Bull is the focal point of the mythical farming village community of Ambridge. The Rovers Return is where the television characters of *Coronation Street* act out the day-to-day dramas of a working-class area of Manchester.

...and some have architectural, historical or cultural interest and I think, in hindsight, I learned as much about people, with a pint in my hand, as I did about places, when I walked. So read on, if you will, without keeping count!

If you are mathematically minded, you will have gathered that thirty-nine million is an exaggeration! The real figure, I suppose, could be nearer two million, because the entire route was just over a thousand miles. Measure your own stride if you like, or count your paces as you walk a measured mile but, unless your legs are Colossally[7] long, or you just happen to be a 'sub 4' qualifier in the Roger Bannister[8] mould, I'd be surprised if you can cover the distance in much less than two thousand paces, or fifteen minutes. There's a challenge for you! Try it again with a loaded pack on your back over broken ground and you'll be nearer to working out the exact figure, but who cares? My odyssey through Britain was much more than a certain number of steps.

All of that lay ahead of me as the countdown to the summer holidays began. The last few weeks in an academic year are busy and, with the children either tired or excited (or both), there are exams and concerts and galas and sports days ...and reports. I hardly had time to have second thoughts – besides which, I had already bought my ticket, so to speak. There would be no turning back, and this particular roller coaster ride was about to begin.

---

[7] Colossus was one of the seven wonders of the ancient world. His statue in Rhodes was about the same size as the Statue of Liberty.

[8] Roger Bannister was the first athlete to run a mile in under four minutes, something which was generally thought to be impossible.

CHAPTER 1

Land's End – The Tamar Valley

IN WHICH
...a rocky start, more than just one close shave and brushes with a gunman and nudists lead to some unexpected animal encounters. I wonder if I will ever get out of Cornwall.

Term broke up for the summer holidays. It had been an unusual last day for me, starting early, onstage, having a sponsored 'blade nought' over my head and beard, in front of a hundred or so excited pupils and curious parents. As I thanked Mr Christophi for at least having left my eyebrows behind, I confess to wondering whether the stunt was worth it ... not for my own part (actually I recommend a head shave, particularly if, like me, you find yourself follicly challenged) but because my shocking appearance was enough to reduce Isabella, my daughter, to tears! I tried to reassure her that it was still me, then reassured myself that the scalping had actually attracted quite a bit in additional sponsorship. A colleague asked flippantly if I'd thought about having fifty lashes, too, or something else out of *Tom Brown's School Days*![9]

After a glass of the headmaster's champagne with the staff and an impromptu tea with friends, I set about packing. As neighbours dropped in to wish me well, my mind was racing and I remember feeling inside how I imagine brides-to-be must feel at 'T minus two hours'. I made a big effort to calm down and, in the end, my packing was so cool and collected that I missed the train I'd hoped would

---

[9] *Tom Brown's School Days* is an 1857 novel by Thomas Hughes. It describes life at Rugby School, where Tom is beaten and burned by his nemesis Flashman, a bully. The book has been made into several films and TV adaptations.

take me to London! Instead, we drove to Victoria Coach Station. I waved goodbye to a tearful family trio and, with a lump in my throat, boarded the bus westward bound.

The first man I met was, appropriately enough, named Adam. He got on at Heathrow and sat alongside. Adam flouted the regulation about liquor on the buses: he offered me a slurp of Scotch. It seemed impolite not to accept (although I'd told myself that I wouldn't have any whisky until north of the border and my next 'dram' wasn't until Aberdour in Fife). He taught me a variant of poker and I won all of the first few hands. Beginners' luck... or a portent of success ahead? I wondered. Or was he about to say: "Now let's make it a tenner a trick" and hustle me dry?

"I never gamble," was what he actually said. I was mightily relieved but, in truth, not as relieved as I was when he got out, at Taunton, for the sole, selfish reason that for the rest of the night ride I could stretch out my tense body over both seats. Several times I closed my eyes, not really expecting much. Such was the excitement that golden sleep was never going to charm me for hours that night but, even so, I can only faintly recollect the scenes at the various staging posts along the way. The overcoated people who waited, either standing around under artificial light with luggage and cigarettes, or else behind the wheels of carefully positioned and dimly lit cars nearby, could have been at Newton Abbot, Plymouth, Liskeard, St Austell or Truro ...I couldn't be sure. Occasionally, I caught sight of a road sign, invariably showing that Penzance was still a long way off, and triggering thoughts which began: "If it's taking the bus, travelling at this speed this long, however long is it going to take me..." But I would dismiss the calculations and try more a little more 'shut-eye'.

By the time we reached the terminus at Penzance it was broad daylight and I had no difficulty in identifying my rucksack from the remaining luggage unceremoniously offloaded by the burly driver.

"Blimey! What you got in there, the Crown Jewels?"

CHAPTER 1: LAND'S END – THE TAMAR VALLEY

It costs just 5p to go into the supervised and spotless Gents, where there were lashings of hot water and, after a night on the road, I think it was one of the best investments I made on the trip. Splashing the water over my face, I paused for a moment with my hands over my eyes and contemplated the scale of what I had set myself. Now there were butterflies in my stomach!

Land's End is only about nine miles from Penzance but the local charabanc visits every cove and disused tin mine in the district, and takes at least two hours. There is now a theme park where, as a child, I remember only a coach park… but the scenery is just the same. I threaded my way through the park and followed a path down to where I could watch the Atlantic waves smashing up the rock faces at the very tip of England. Of the many things whizzing around inside my head, I remember being struck by a paradox: The 'constants' in this changing landscape were the water, in perpetual motion, and the land. Britain is not of a particular and timeless form and shape. I sensed it at that time, just there and, as I was to become increasingly aware, overgrown here, eroded there, the land itself is as dynamic an entity as can be.

It was approaching midday when I took my first snaps and registered my challenge in the 'End to Enders' book kept in the bar of the Land's End Hotel. I wrote:

"Jonathan Richards from Aberdour School in Surrey, walking to John o' Groats, via Aberdour in Fife, for the Imperial Cancer Research Fund. If Beefy Botham can do it, so can I …(I hope!)"

Visitors to Land's End or John o' Groats will know that you can have your picture taken in front of a signpost which you can customise in the way that the churchwarden changes the numbers of hymns for the day.

"Aberdour 680," I instructed, and the characters were duly slotted into place, pointing broadly north-east. I posed for the snap and, after something traditionally Cornish from the cafeteria, I was off.

Land's End – rugged cliffs at the very tip.

CHAPTER 1: LAND'S END – THE TAMAR VALLEY

The sea mist was lifting as I set out along the peninsular path. Before long, the inviting view of Whitesands Bay opened out. At Land's End, it simply hadn't been safe to get down to the sea itself, but here I really could dip a toe into the Atlantic. The beach was practically deserted and I savoured the moment. I wondered if I would find any other comparable places. Though seeming a devil of a long way off, I imagined that beaches in the sparsely populated far north of Scotland might well fit the bill. It would be up to me to see if I could find out!

I found a path leading back up to the road and, almost immediately met a brigade of firemen walking, proudly, fast and in uniform the other way, complete with backup vehicle and collecting buckets.

"Going all the way?" one asked as we passed. I smiled.

"It's a long way, you know," he called back to me. I did know but not, I was sure, experientially, as he did. I hoped that that depth of knowledge would be mine before long.

There is very bright light in Cornwall, although going from south to north means that the sun (and prevailing winds) are mostly at your back. With the sun shining pleasantly on the patch of exposed skin between the top of the rucksack and my cap, I walked all afternoon along paths and across farmland, coming, in time, to the Penzance youth hostel. (The signpost is not immediately obvious, being slightly out of the way and screened by trees.) I asked a lady for confirmation that I was heading the right way. She smiled kindly:

"Yes, dear, not far to go now." In one sense, I reflected, she was not wrong … After all it was now less than a thousand miles!

You can be a youth hosteller at any age and I'd planned to make use of this budget accommodation along the way… but not at this establishment. I merely wanted to renew my membership. Unfortunately, it was mid-afternoon and the hostel was closed. While I was reading a notice on the door, a group of German students approached and, grasping the situation I have to say rather quicker than I had, opportunistically asked me to mind their bags while they went to the beach! They were carrying quite a lot of luggage and I could see why they wanted to shed some. The only German I know comes from Brahms' *Requiem*[10] and it took a little while to convince them that I wasn't staying around.

It felt like being on holiday as, in the evening sunshine, I strolled along the beach at Longrock to St Michael's Mount. Although tempted, I hadn't paddled at Whitesands earlier in the day. Here I did, to cool my feet but, on peeling off a sock, I was genuinely surprised to find a plump blister on my heel.

I had made sure that my boots were broken in nicely before I set off. In hindsight, I think even broken-in boots blister you to begin with, if you walk all day with a full pack, and that it must take time for one's feet to toughen. I remembered various pieces of advice given to me whilst I planned, much of it contradictory but, on the subject of blisters, several people had told me that treatment must be immediate. If blisters are ignored, problems may arise. I had an excellent first aid kit and carried out the first of many puncture repair operations. In fact, over the first week or so, I spent more time fiddling with my feet than I spent doing anything else save walking, sleeping and rehydrating in various Cornish watering holes.

Excluding a fleeting visit to the bar in the Land's End Hotel, my first watering hole was to be the Mount View Hotel. Unintentionally, I drew attention to myself shuffling through the door (which slammed shut behind me) and one of the four drinkers at the bar interrupted his game of cards to ask:

"So what are you up to?"

It was a question that could be taken in more than one way. I plumped for a straightforward reply:

"I'm walking to John o' Groats."

---

[10] Johannes Brahms composed *Ein deutsches Requiem* between 1865 and 1868. It is the composer's longest work and it broke the convention of Latin language settings of the Requiem Mass for the dead.

CHAPTER 1: LAND'S END – THE TAMAR VALLEY

It felt good to articulate the affirmation, now that truly I was on my way. Considering where we were, I imagined that the lads must have seen my like before. Even so, they appeared interested and, from the moment I dumped my rucksack in a corner and pulled up a stool, they engaged me in lively chat. I have heard that there are unemployment 'black spots' in parts of Cornwall but, judging by these fellows, there is no shortage of talent. Having quickly established that I was walking for charity, they devised and presented to me a personal business plan for effective fundraising en route. In the preceding months, I had given considerable thought as to how best to raise sponsorship. Unlike the firemen and celebrity walkers, I was not accompanied by teams of bucket shakers – nor had I planned to pass through the great centres of population (in fact, the opposite). I knew that the bulk of my sponsorship would have to arise from different sources. Like all the best ideas, theirs was simple:

"You're obviously going to be stopping for a drink from time to time…" (He was not wrong.) "… How many pubs and bars are there between here and John o' Groats?" It was a mind-boggling thought.

"All you have to do is ask for a pound whenever you stop, and it will snowball. You'll see."

From inside my rucksack, we took a fresh sponsorship form, which was duly endorsed with the hotel's stamp, and each of the four contributed a pound to an original capital fund. As they predicted, it was to grow exponentially at a rate which would be the envy even of investment bankers. One condition was made: that I send them a postcard from John o' Groats, which seemed eminently fair to me. I was even given a stamp! And, before I left, I received something else – advice and directions to a campsite about five miles along the way.

I trod gingerly at first, but a far bigger problem for me than my solitary blister, at that time, in spite of the directions I'd received, was path finding. What may, at one time, have been an ancient right of way could quite possibly be a mass of head-high brambles and vicious stingers, completely impassable. This sort of thing forced me to change my planned route. I had already done so, when I picked a path down to the beach at Whitesands but it still surprises me that, after such careful planning, I began changing tracks so readily and also that, having set the precedent, I continued to change plans, throughout the length of Britain, whenever the whim took me. On the other hand, an early *enforced* diversion was when a herd of young bullocks cornered me (and my bright red rucksack) against a stone wall. In the end I had to jump over, and landed in a thorn bush. Surely things would get easier, I told myself.

I found the campsite, which was on a farm, and a sound sleep was ended by a peacock who was strutting around, proud of his plumage and also of his voice. The shrill squawk was much louder than a cockerel's and certainly most effective as an alarm call. Unfortunately, unlike my alarm clock at home, he couldn't be turned off, although a permanent solution did come to mind!

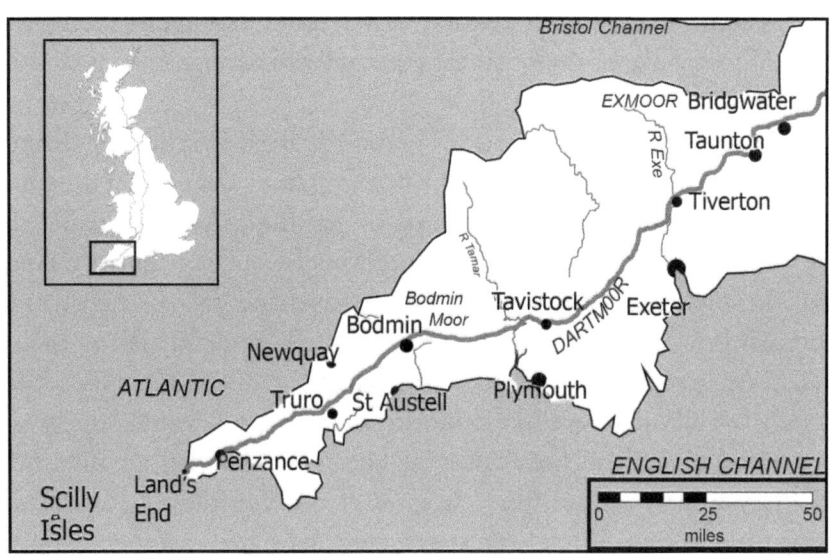

West Country Blister Miles.

CHAPTER 1: LAND'S END – THE TAMAR VALLEY

No worse than a little bit achy, I packed up and found a string of footpaths heading east. Even with the best maps, it is often difficult to tell, for example, which side of the barn to go. Murphy's Law[11] seemed to be applying itself when, doubling back for the fourth or fifth time that morning (and treading through some pretty sloppy stuff, too, I remember) I came face to face with the farmer, with his gun.

"Goin' far?" he asked.

"Pretty far" – a response I'd prepared earlier and I asked directions to the next village. With his ruddy complexion and deep blue eyes he may well have been what people think of as a typical Cornishman, but I'm not so sure that such a thing exists. Accents are another matter, however, for his was undiluted and unmistakable… and I enjoyed his lilting burr.

The farmer told me a story about how one day he had seen a dog running over his land, off the lead. He fired a "warning shot" across its bows before the dog's owners appeared just behind the animal. The shot only narrowly missed them. They were blind, the dog was a guide dog and they had walked from John o' Groats to raise money for Guide Dogs for the Blind. I counted my blessings – one of which was not to have received a warning shot – and pressed on.

Following local tracks and walled lanes in the company of blue butterflies and bees at the bright pink, hardy wild fuchsias, I meandered into and through Camborne and Redruth, towns with a history in tin mining but for me, familiar territory from more recent times. Cornish hospitality, together with the availability of the very strong beer known as H.S.D., which stands for Hicks Special Draught but is more usually known as "High Speed Death" or "Death" for short, made this part of England an ideal location for several happy cricket tours. For old times' sake (and to develop the sponsorship

---

[11] Murphy's Law: "Anything which can go wrong will go wrong", or "When nothing can go wrong, it will".

fund) I checked out a few of the local landmarks and then put best foot forward again, wondering with each successive stop why the rucksack seemed so much heavier!

Apart from daylight, the other thing that had gradually dawned on me on the coach journey west was that Cornwall is a devil of a long county. If you have ever had the misfortune to sit in a traffic jam on the A30 on what West Country hoteliers refer to as "Changeover Day" you will know what I mean – but look on the map if you don't believe me. I looked on the map, one which showed the whole of Britain. I'd walked for about forty miles from Land's End and yet it seemed as if I had hardly got anywhere …a couple of centimetres on a map as big as the groundsheet of my tent.

My blisters were multiplying, particularly on my right foot. (The reason, I later realised, was that walking the cambered lanes on the right, i.e. towards the occasional tractor, was slowly but surely pushing my weight towards the outside edge of my right boot.) I kept myself going by marching to music in my head. If things got painful, downhill usually, I would sing loudly and, in the deserted lanes, not many people would have heard me. I counted paces per minute, because it helped to keep a steady rhythm, so that going uphill, my stride was shorter but no slower. I also counted miles 'under the belt' and even more intently, days and hours past, partly for the reason that long-distance walkers say that if you are still going after two weeks, your body and feet will have reacted to what is expected of them, and you will find things less hard. So I remember singing to myself: "Eleven more days to go, eleven more days of sorrow…"

My second (and rather less 'pain-free') night was spent on a caravan site near Truro. My mind went back to student days when I performed, with thirty-nine friends, Tallis' forty-part motet "Spem in alium" in the cathedral, which is almost certainly the Duchy's most impressive building. In the morning, whilst humming bits of the bass line, my attention was arrested when I passed an abandoned

CHAPTER 1: LAND'S END – THE TAMAR VALLEY

removal van, parked by the road at the edge of a plot earmarked for an out-of-town shopping development. The van was being used as a giant noticeboard, its message damming developers and planners for killing local business. Tourism, I reminded myself, is Cornwall's biggest business, bigger than farming or fishing and, nowadays, far bigger than mining or porcelain. There was nothing I could do to turn back the clock but, I mused, at least this tourist was supporting Cornish industry, and I resolved to invest in a clotted cream tea at the next opportunity! But was I ever going to get out of Cornwall, I wondered. One of my senior pupils had scornfully predicted "a Cornish capitulation" for me. In fact, I was pleased that he had: I definitely was not prepared to prove him right and that thought alone was enough to distract me from worrying about blisters.

My route took me past the so-called "Cornish Alps", which are huge piles of waste clay and sand from the English China clay mines in the St Austell district and on, up, down, around and along more walled lanes linking village to village.

That afternoon I completely ran out of drink. I was a long way from anywhere and the sun was as hot as it was all summer. Like pennies from heaven, a belly full of sweet and juicy wild strawberries appeared and saw me through to the town of St Columb Major. In that place I played pétanque[12] in the backyard of an excellent pub called The Silver Ball. I was glad to talk to the locals: for one thing, they told me that those parts were completely different from West Cornwall (which made me feel as if I was getting somewhere) and they put me straight on the matter of the campsite I had identified, from the maps, as my resting place for the night.

"You don't want to go there," they said. "It's a nudist camp!"

---

[12] Pétanque is a French game also known as 'boules'. You toss or roll hollow steel balls as close as possible to a small wooden 'piglet' or 'jack'. The deliciously onomatopoeic name actually comes from the Provençal *pès tancats* which means 'planted feet', which is how you must be when you toss the ball.

Luckily, I found a nearby alternative but had another scare in the morning when, on Bodmin Moor, I had unintentionally strayed off a not so well beaten track and, in acid bog with scorched gorse bushes misshapen by prevailing winds, I had a close encounter with an adder. This was no ordinary snake in the grass but a very rare black adder. An expert back in school confirmed its identification. She, for it was a female snake, was tightly curled into a coil about the size of the frying pan I use for making curry. I practically trod on the snake and it straightened itself to a metre or more, before sloping off without seeking confrontation. Not for the last time on my journey, I looked around a remote and unpopulated area wondering, "What would I do if...?"

I headed east towards the River Tamar, which I crossed at Gunnislake. On that day I remember thinking that although I had walked about 100 miles I was still only a tenth of the way to John o' Groats. I was beginning to understand what the fireman had meant.

CHAPTER 2

The Tamar Valley – The Mendips

IN WHICH
…With a little help from my friends, old and new, I cross 'cider country'. In the footsteps of a Saxon king, I come across some modern Saxons and inadvertently gatecrash a wedding.

At the bottom of the long ascent out of the Tamar Valley a fellow pulled up, in his converted ambulance, to offer me a lift. I didn't hesitate: "No, thank you, I'm walking all the way." He didn't stop to question but, twenty-five or thirty minutes later, I was still toiling up the same hill and wondered if perhaps he was halfway across Dartmoor by then.

The moor was my next objective. I'd been offered a bed with friends who live near Tavistock. To say that I enjoyed a bath there would be an understatement on a par with Michael Fish's October '87 forecast for some strong winds in the Channel.[13]

I complained to my friend, a very experienced climber and walker, that my rucksack seemed far too heavy. Going through it he told me about how he had carried a seventy-pound pack on an expedition up a glacier in Iceland.

"You don't need this, you don't need that. What on earth is this?"

Amongst the items he slung out, I recall, were long trousers, which

---

[13] Michael Fish was a long-standing BBC weatherman. On the 15th of October 1987 he said in a broadcast: "Earlier on today, apparently, a woman rang the BBC and said she heard there was a hurricane on the way… Well, if you're watching, don't worry, there isn't!" That evening, the worst storm to hit South-East England for three centuries caused record damage and killed 19 people.

I missed only once, all my spare socks ("Who's going to complain?" he asked), T-shirts (from then on, I wore my marvellous sweat-busting thermal vests) my cooker ("You won't starve in Britain – have it back north of Inverness"), a foam pad supplied by my mother which I had been using as a pillow – it was meant for kneeling on, perhaps when weeding the garden or if moved to sudden prayer whilst walking on cobbles ("Come on, Jo!" he cried in disbelief) – and several maps of Cornwall (you need about forty OS maps in all to go from Land's End to John o' Groats, though not all at once). My compass was found to be 162 degrees in error, so that went, as did my insect repellent which I did miss, sorely, in Scotland, and most of my first aid kit.

"Triangular bandage?" he cried. "You'll never need that!" Little did he know!

In all, Henry must have reduced the mass of my pack by about 5 kgs but his wife gave me about 10 kgs of sandwiches and home-made fruit cake.

Walking with me, and avoiding bogs and firing ranges, Henry navigated as far as the tourist stop at Postbridge. We shook hands and I pressed on alone again, via The Postbridge Inn, The Warren House Inn and the bleak and windy open moor, to Moretonhampstead. I camped 'wild' on some high ground and spent a couple of hours eating sandwiches, listening to the wind howling, before drifting off into a misty sleep to dream of Baskerville hounds.[14]

The next day was the first of my big mile-munchers. I came down from the moor, through Tedburn St Mary and Crediton, along the Exe Valley to Tiverton. This was one week into the walk and a pattern was developing of walk and rest. Typically, I would start early and not stop for three or four hours, by which time I would have clocked off around ten miles. I would rest, sitting on my rucksack in the corner

---

[14] In *The Hound of the Baskervilles* (1901-02) by Sir Arthur Conan Doyle, Sherlock Holmes investigates attempted murder inspired by a mythical diabolic hound. The story is set on Dartmoor.

CHAPTER 2: THE TAMAR VALLEY – THE MENDIPS

Whitesands Bay

Ponies on Dartmoor.

of a field, study the map or read for a few minutes, and then walk for another three hours or so. If I could find a nice country pub, all the better, but then I would eat, lots. The point was that most of my day's walking had to be done before I stopped to eat. With good weather, i.e. not too hot, I might continue for another five hours or so. I was becoming deeply conscious of the relationship between time and distance. The mathematics came to life ... ten hours of three miles per hour equals thirty miles, or another centimetre on the map of Britain!

There is a picturesque canal from Tiverton towards Taunton. The first mile or two along the towpath is popular with tourists, local folk and, I can tell you, with a certain courting student in years gone by. I don't know much about hypnosis but there is definitely a sense in which long-distance walking is similar. The metric plod, plod, plod, plod is ever present. By the restful waters of the canal the slowly shifting visual images were taking me back in time – and this was an experience I felt at many times during my journey. Perhaps this sounds odd but it's different from when, for example, you drive past the place you were married or used to go to the cinema. One's memory is jogged, but the moment is passed by the time one reaches the next traffic lights. In my situation, there were hours and hours to think and reflect.

Mid-afternoon, I had to stop daydreaming and concentrate on route finding, because the canal becomes unnavigable and the cross-country route into Somerset is not clear. I paused before rolling under an electric fence, not out of timidity over the low-voltage shock I might get through my bulky pack, but because there was a bull the size of a tank on the other side. There were heifers, too, and I rightly guessed that he was preoccupied. Even so, my crossing of the field was hasty.

A peel of bells came from the next village. My footpath went straight to the churchyard gates and I emerged from a gap in the hedge precisely as the happy couple were being showered in confetti immediately across the narrow lane. "Who's that bloke in all the photos?" people will wonder. I retired to a discreet distance and met two telephone engineers who had 'knocked off' and were watching everybody. One of them wanted to come with me, then and there. His mate had to persuade him not to, but the first was very keen:

"Couldn't I just go as far as Taunton? You could pick me up in town."

After some reasoning, I left the village alone and made for the county town, camping to the north on a cider farm.

"Eighty pence for two litres," I remember the woman in charge saying, before adding something which was more a guarantee than a disclaimer:

"It's strong, mark you. You'll sleep well tonight, my lover"... and I did!

In the morning she recharged my flagon (at a specially discounted rate) and I set off along another canal, towards Bridgwater. This was high summer. There may have been a dozen or more species of dragonfly on that stretch of water, in abundance, especially the little ones which shine, electric blue ... And in the meadows alongside, an array of wild flowers in bloom made the setting idyllic. There were pretty large numbers of recreational cyclists, too. They came past, mostly in twos and almost invariably they came back the other way.

"Hello again!" I would find myself saying. I guessed that, depending on the time lapse between the cyclist's outward and inward passings, I could gauge the distance to the canalside pub which was undoubtedly their destination and turning point. So, if I saw the same people within the space of an hour or so, I was encouraged.

In Bridgwater, a brass band played in the park. I lay down on the warm grass and closed my eyes. They played competently arranged medleys with tunes like 'It's a long way to Tipperary'. I joined in, singing quietly, on my back. 'It's a long way to John o' Groats...' But, realising that my final destination didn't scan very well, I changed it to 'It's a Long Way to Aberdour', which fitted better and it was true – about another five hundred miles by my route until I would meet up with my school's Scottish namesake in the Kingdom of Fife. "Come on, JR," I thought to myself, "you had better get on with it, then."

At a petrol station on the main road I stopped to buy a couple of cold drinks. Loading the spare into my rucksack, which I had propped up behind the low wall at the edge of the forecourt, I was bending over the wall and rustling around in the cavernous compartments, when a soft voice came from behind me:

"Hello." I wondered if she was talking to me. "Hello there!" I stood up.

"Yes?" I enquired, in a teacher's voice. The young mother blushed, paused, then continued.

"I thought you were being sick!" We laughed and I thanked her for her concern.

A little while later I crossed the M5. I looked back westward from the bridge and surveyed the caravan of caravans Bristol bound. From my lofty vantage point, the highway stretched for miles into the dim distance and, for the first time since Land's End, I felt a sense of satisfaction. Yes, I had really walked all that way, but ever-mindful of the challenge ahead, I turned my back to the setting sun and continued across more fields towards the Somerset village of Cossington.

Following a disused railway track, I frightened bunnies near the watercourse known as King's Sedgemoor Drain. Upstream, by a pedestrian bridge, I had stopped and was pawing over my maps when I became aware that a couple of local girls, in middle or late-teens, were making ready for an evening swim. They had not seen me, and were in fits of giggles. Naturally, I averted my gaze and only looked up from my study of contours when the larger of the two screamed for help. There was little doubt that the water was a shock, but she was not drowning, only yelping because of the cold!

CHAPTER 2: THE TAMAR VALLEY – THE MENDIPS

The Red Tile in Cossington, in my view, is certainly one of the best pubs in Britain. What you need, I reckon, is somewhere that has excellent food, beautiful barmaids, and very well kept beer, with no jukeboxes, video games or piped music, and where all the smoke goes up the chimneys of large, open fireplaces; if the landlord is a cricketer, all the better. It seemed to me that The Red Tile fitted that description rather well. The cricketers were drinking after a game. I think that they must have won, although they struck me as being the kind of folk who wouldn't mind if they had lost ... and they definitely wouldn't have let anything like that dampen spirits in the bar. I felt uplifted by their friendliness and I resolved to return there one day, with my family.

That night I stayed in the village with Aunt Grace, retired headmistress of the local school. She is not my aunt, or any close relative, but she is known in the family and – having taught everyone in the pub and their parents – seemed to be everybody's aunt. Apparently, she has a ninety-year-old boyfriend who drives a Rolls-Royce. People spoke of her with respect and affection and when I met her it was easy to see why. Inside her chocolate box cottage, which was smothered in climbing roses, she was happy to tell me about village life and, particularly, about education over the years. "Children today have no manners or respect," she explained, blaming the parents, TV and the teaching profession itself, for becoming too liberal. Who was I to disagree?

In the morning, I set off across the Somerset Levels. Over the years, many drainage ditches have been excavated to improve the marshy land. I didn't previously know that the word 'Somerset' comes from 'somer saeta', which means 'the land of the summer people', because in winter, widespread flooding made much of the land inaccessible. There are many paths which follow alongside the rhynes, but if you try to cross a field diagonally, as I did, you can get literally bogged down. I recollected having made, with children, a giant model of the marsh at Athelney, when I was teaching how King Alfred followed marsh people along a secret path to dry ground. There was something about burnt cakes, too.[15]

It was another burning hot day. The sun was high and the air was still. By mid-morning I was already feeling as parched as a character from *Lawrence of Arabia*[16] when, for the second time since I began my trip, there came miraculous relief from my thirst. The angel of mercy came in human form, a farmer aged between sixty-five and a hundred and twenty. He was wrinkled, as brown as a berry, and his name was Hector.

"Hoy!" came the voice from behind a hedge. "Hoy!"

He gestured me towards a barn saying that he had something for me to try. The cool inside the barn hit me with exactly the opposite effect of leaving an air-conditioned airport lounge when you first step out into a hot place, and it was so dark that it took my eyes a moment or two to adjust. My pupils widened as I made out a number of huge cider casks. Cobwebbed beams supported the structure, and vintage farm machinery, of the kind that you sometimes see fixed to walls in pubs, lay in dark corners and were propped up against the woodwork. Mr Hector scuttled off to wash up a glass, pushing newspapers and rags or something off a chair for me. His own seat was an old and wide oak carver, solidly positioned between two barrels. He drew me off a small tumbler. The liquid was a rich straw colour, not the least cloudy and positively steamed as it bubbled out of the wood. I thanked him most profusely and then downed it in one draft. The 'Zider' was sharp and dry and burnt like ginger wine on the way

---

[15] In the year 878 the Anglo-Saxon King Alfred fled from invading Vikings to the Somerset Levels. The story goes that, preoccupied with his battle plans, he allowed some cakes to burn, and was roundly scolded by the woman in whose house he had taken refuge.

[16] Peter O'Toole starred along with Alec Guinness, Jack Hawkins, Anthony Quinn and Omar Sharif in the epic film of 1962.

down. The farmer said nothing, watching me drink. He didn't need a verdict but simply asked: "Would ye like a drop more?"

His smile was broad and gave a clear view of his three or four remaining yellow and black teeth and I noticed that his eyes pointed in different directions. This time he drew off two glasses, then sat back in his chair.

On the subject of traditional cider making, in which field Mr Hector is an undoubted expert, spiders and pruning, I was told, are what it takes! I knew that skilful pruning of fruit trees produces a better crop but I was perplexed about the spiders. Apparently, their webs catch the 'vinegar fly' which, if left unchecked, can quickly ruin the cider. I felt sure that he was glad of the company – and it was fascinating to learn about the cider, Somerset life and how things were when he was a boy. A couple of times I got up to go, but he easily convinced me that it was too hot outside to bother with walking just then.

When, eventually, I did say goodbye, I glanced at my watch and understood precisely what is meant by the saying 'time flies when you're enjoying yourself' and I knew that there was no way I was going to reach the Bristol area that day, as I had hoped. The cider, however, had had a mellowing effect, and I'm sure I would have shrugged my shoulders nonchalantly as if to say "so what" to myself, if it were possible to do so, carrying a massive rucksack.

I was floating along a completely deserted track when once more I heard a voice. It was indistinct and seemed to be coming from the air, but I wasn't imagining things. There it was again. Like Samuel, I as ready to reply: "Yes, master, here I am,"[17] when I made out a few words:

"Vikings … twelve points … competitors."

I was still confused and remained so for at least two miles, by

---

[17] From the Old Testament, 1 Samuel 3:4.

which time the voice was clear and I had realised what was going on. It was a primary school's sports day and the voice drifting so far across the Levels was presumably the headmaster's, over a very loud tannoy.

The Vikings were one of four teams. I think the others were Saxons, Romans and Celts, but I remember being able to follow events quite clearly for about an hour. It is said that Englishmen back the underdog and I can confirm that instinctively I was pleased when Saxon boys came in first and second in the Year 5 sack race to bring their team back into contention. I had, as so often during those salad days, time to reflect on my own philosophy. I thought in this instance how good it is when children are encouraged to 'have a go' in diverse areas of the curriculum, and how often people discover hidden talents if they do so. As I walked on past the school I tried to work out when I had first felt that way and recalled organising a class assembly when the unlikely stars had been a very naughty and disruptive girl and a hyperactive boy with a mania for fiddling with things. We put on a Shakespearean-style show and these two children, to general astonishment, revealed themselves to be masterly entertainers in the fields of expressive dance and juggling, respectively.

I made a brief food stop at The Trotter Inn at Crickham, where I attempted to reorientate myself by asking directions. The farmers couldn't agree as to the best way to head out of the village, i.e. down the lane or across the fields, so I thanked both parties and left them to it, plumping for the tarmacked lane!

I followed the roads into Cheddar, which was bustling, as I had expected, and then headed out again, up and over the Mendips. I chose a string of footpaths, rather than the famous road up the gorge, which is arguably better experienced in a car. Progress was better and I allowed myself the occasional self-congratulatory look over my shoulder across miles and miles of West Country. Now, I knew, England was opening up.

CHAPTER 3

The Mendips – The Malverns

IN WHICH
*…the march continues, across marshes and Mendips. After
a couple of embarrassing situations, I land on my feet.
There are more meanders and more blisters (although my
own recede) but I soon have something else to worry about.*

I was keen to push ahead. Unfortunately, it was getting late and my maps showed neither sign of any campsite nor any obvious wild area in which to pitch. I needn't have worried, for in the village of West Harptree the publican at The Crown asked me if I would like to 'camp' in the beer garden – an invitation which he made immediately upon my entry to the bar and without the least prompting. I thanked him and swiftly erected my Eurohike near a wall dripping in clematis and jasmine.

My tent had a front zipper, which was closed, with me inside. I had unpacked and was reading or resting, I forget which, when I became faced with an unusual dilemma. A couple had come into the garden and were having their drinks at a table nearby. It was evident from the increasing intimacy of their conversation that they believed they were alone, as indeed they were, apart from me, quietly concealed in my tent. The problem was that I needed the loo – besides which I was ravenously hungry and didn't want to miss the nine o'clock deadline for food at the bar. How was I to make my exit without embarrassing them and myself? I thought about coughing loudly but, instead, boldly unzipped myself and clambered out. The lovers did look flushed. I said something like "Excuse me" to which she confirmed that she'd thought there was nobody in the tent and he said he thought I was a New Age traveller. I scuttled inside to some more cider and a bowl of lasagne, over which I chatted with locals, played skittles and was invited to a wedding! In the morning the landlord's wife got up early to cook me a full breakfast, for which she wouldn't take payment. Instead, she sent me on my way with a sweet Somersetshire kiss.

It was another scorcher, that day. For all I knew, Mike Atherton's England cricketers might have been receiving an Aussie bashing at Lord's,[18] but so isolated from current affairs was I, and so focused on my own business, that I hardly gave other people a thought. I hadn't even heard anything about the blossoming romance of a certain tragic princess and the son of a Knightsbridge shopkeeper, for example. I was preoccupied with making up some lost time, as I had set up rendezvous further along ... not least my lift back from John o' Groats ... which I didn't want to miss.

I crossed the A37 and took the opportunity to buy some more drink from a petrol station. It was probably about ten o'clock and another customer, wearing only swimming trunks (that's how hot it was) asked me what I was up to. He told me he had seen me in Cheddar the previous day. Could he sponsor me? ... and why didn't I have a sign on my back? He then remembered he hadn't got a bean on him. I thanked him for the thought, resolved to make myself a sign next time I got to a computer, and left wondering how he was going to pay for his petrol – credit card, I supposed.

My own fuel is sold in pints and not litres and I was taking a little on-board in Keynsham, a suburb of Bristol in an inn, The London, where, with my arrival, the bar staff outnumbered the customers by a total of two to one, the employees being a leggy blonde and a more petite brunette. My feet were very tender and I practically rooted to a soft chair near the pool table. All I was doing was sitting, sipping

---

[18] Lord's Cricket Ground in London is the spiritual home of cricket. Mike Atherton was the captain of England in 1997.

and thinking. Perhaps it was the boredom, or else the heat, which had got to the girls but, for no apparent reason, they began giggling. I glanced across and I'm not sure if it was a good thing or not, because the barmaids, still giggling, were attempting to distract me from my contemplations by acting out their version of some seduction scene. It reminded me of the bit in the Paul Newman film *Cool Hand Luke*,[19] where a Southern girl tries to wind up the prisoners by polishing a car, using more than her soapy sponge to make bubbles. These two local hotties started by polishing the beer pumps, in a fashion that left very little to the imagination… and while the taller girl moved on to the fruit machine, using her chest rather more than the cloth, the other continued to work rhythmically on one of the pumps, hand over hand, up and down the pump shaft, huffing condensing breath onto the brass knobble at its top, whenever she sensed I might have noticed. Like Luke, I stayed cool (taking the odd sip)… right up to the moment when they both approached to begin work on the pool table, right in front of me. Surprisingly (or perhaps not) the pair came around my side but chose to polish the already gleaming chrome rails on the other side of the table. The wiggling movements were a little too much, and I suddenly felt the urgent need of fresh air. My pulse was racing, I was no longer thinking about my sore feet, and there was yet more giggling, as I darted for the door. I quickly found a post office and wrote a postcard to my wife!

That day I walked as far as Chipping Sodbury, which is an old market town that has grown and grown. I was discovering that, in residential areas, it is difficult to find places to camp and, not wishing to be 'moved along', or else charged with vagrancy, I decided to find a 'B and B'. I tried a couple of places, which were full, and then went into a hotel. I asked at the bar and the lady disappeared to check:

---

[19] Directed by Stuart Rosenberg, *Cool Hand Luke* is a US prison film drama from 1967.

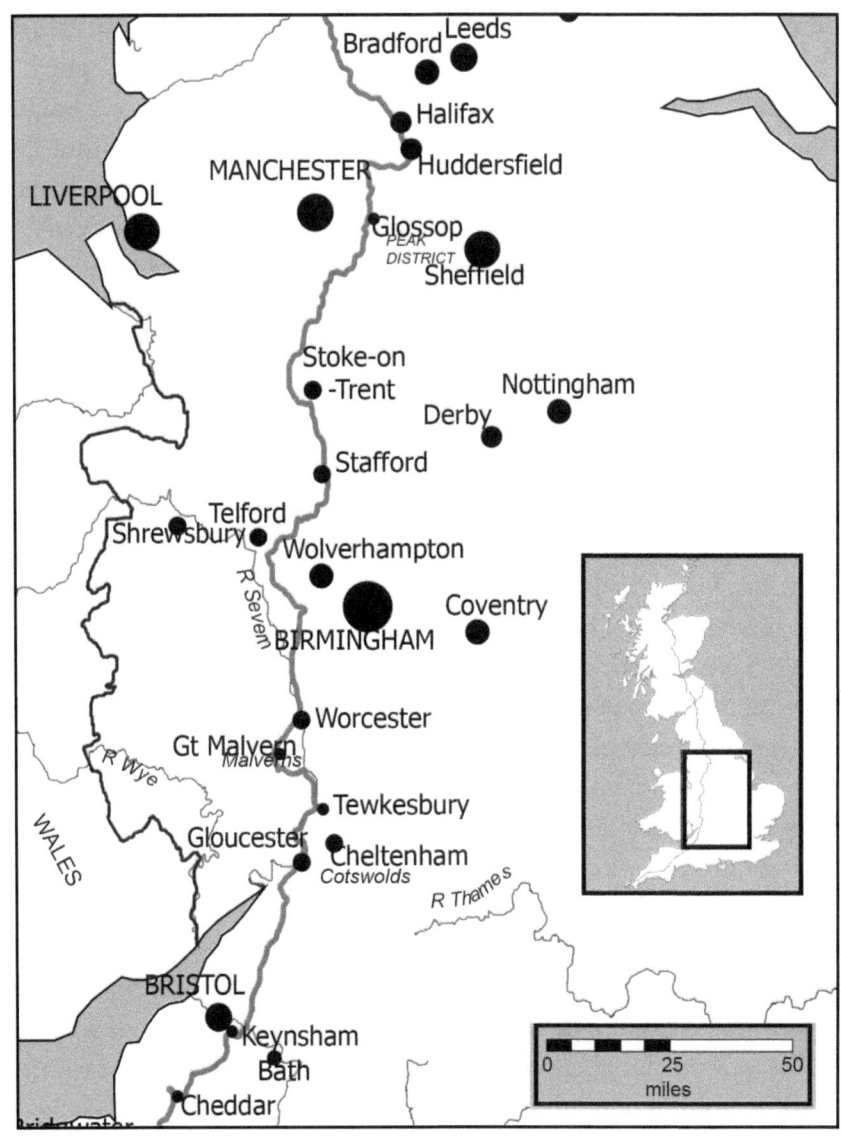

Through England's Heart.

CHAPTER 3: THE MENDIPS – THE MALVERNS

"We do have a room," she said, "thirty-nine pounds fifty."

Thinking that this was more than I wanted to pay and wondering if I could find a field to the north, I was being indecisive when someone at the bar turned around, saying:

"I know where you can stay," and, to his mates, "He could stay with us, couldn't he?"

These lads were real-life characters from *Auf Wiedersehen, Pet*[20] working on a pipeline, away from home. They were radiographers, whose contracts took them all over the place and wherever gas lines needed to be x-rayed for leaks. They were renting a large 'semi', to the south of town and, if I didn't mind the mess, I was welcome… only I'd have to wait because they were going to have a few drinks first. I said that I wouldn't mind the mess and together we embarked on a crawl of Chipping Sodbury.

I learned that they went out drinking every night but they also worked hard and long hours. As a group they appeared very close, although their backgrounds were certainly not. It may sound like the beginning of a joke, but there was a Scouser, a Geordie, a Yorkshireman and the fourth, who came from Surrey, was teased rotten by the others, on account of his public school accent. It turned out that two of the four were keen on the life of adventure, one having previously walked all 253 miles of the Pennine Way (a challenge which lay ahead for me) and the other whose trekking in the jungles of Africa brought him regularly face to face with creatures with much bigger bites than the odd mosquito which had risked all, when dining out on me, in the marshy Somerset Levels. The lads had set out as four that evening but returned six strong, the other addition being an off-duty barmaid who fell for the charms of an adventurer! Later, back in the house, she took offence when he ignored her for a long time, while he showed

---

[20] *Auf Wiedersehen, Pet* was a 1980s television comedy-drama about the lives of seven construction workers who find employment in Düsseldorf.

me hundreds of spectacular photos of wild animals and country.

It was extremely late when everyone went to bed and extremely early when everyone got up; they had to be onsite by 6.00 am. I was ready to go but they said I could stay as long as I liked:

"Just shut the door on your way out."

I decided to leave when they did but, once I was alone again on the empty road, I reflected on how trusting they had been. I asked myself how relaxed I would have been, meeting an unknown traveller in a bar and within a few hours letting him have the run of my home!

There was more farmland between Sodbury and my next port of call, Wotton-under-Edge. I had arranged to meet the headmaster and his wife for lunch in that town. Mr and Mrs Barraclough would have driven about one hundred and thirty miles east in the time it took me to walk about ten miles north, and we met in the nearest pub to the church with a steeple. I had suggested that particular venue not, as my employer thought, because I had a good knowledge of the area, but because I had a good knowledge of the symbols on Ordnance Survey maps… and guessed that both church and pub would be obvious. In fact, the spire is not the least bit conspicuous, the church is deconsecrated to boot, and there are no pubs within sight! In spite of these potentially frustrating factors, it all worked out fine. We had a large lunch, before walking together up a steep, tunnelled lane to a fine viewpoint looking down onto the town and over South Gloucestershire. Shortly after that place, we parted company. It was certainly good to see familiar faces and the couple of hours we spent together lifted my spirits further.

I was, by that stage, beginning to get into my stride, so to speak, and my blisters were in decline. A woodland path opened out onto grassland at the top of Wotton Hill and my spiritual state approached heady euphoria as I surveyed the stupendous panorama from the Waterloo Plantation.

At that point I was following the Cotswold Way, an excellent trail of

CHAPTER 3: THE MENDIPS – THE MALVERNS

exactly 100 miles that links Bath with Chipping Campden. It is gentle walking for the most part, through woods and fields along clearly defined and waymarked paths. It is difficult to get lost if you follow the 'acorn signs' which designate long-distance pathways, and I was surprised to be stopped by a couple of chaps who had got themselves into a pickle. I had seen the pair in the pub earlier, they were pretty distinctive, being kitted out rather like I was, each one loaded up with a huge rucksack. Then I'd (rightly) assumed that they were walking the length of the Cotswold Way. In the course of my adventure, this was one of the times when, because of where I was, it didn't surprise me to see other walkers. For a reason which is difficult to describe but which I suspect is to do with solidarity, it was rather nice to come across others in the same boat, or should that be boot? Apparently rambling is very popular, but apart from one or two walkers with daysacks on Dartmoor, and the firemen, I hadn't seen much evidence … perhaps the majority have more sense than to set out in a heatwave.

"Where are we?" was the direct question which arrested me. They were businessmen from Essex, probably in their forties. They had taken ten days off work to meet this mid-life challenge. I found myself giving them advice, not just on the route (which was straight ahead) but also in response to their questions about kit and blisters.

"Blisters!" I exclaimed. I was an expert but I grimaced when one of them rolled off his sock. His heel was raw and, had it not been for the crumbs of disintegrated pink loo roll, probably from the pub, stuck to the wound, it wouldn't have looked out of place in the butchery department. "Yuck!" was my less than supportive response as I delved for my Granuflex. I explained how you massage the dressing up to body temperature, before pressing it over the blister. You have to hold it in place for a further minute or two until a chemical bond is formed with the skin.

"What if you haven't got any skin left?" he laughed, with jocular stoicism. I didn't answer but showed him the brand name and reassured them both that it draws the fluid and takes away the pain. I kept a couple of strips for myself and gave him the rest. His need was undoubtedly greater than mine!

"Gawd bless you, guvnor!" he quoted, in exaggerated cockney.

The three of us walked together for a little way. I remember being asked if I thought they would make it to Chipping Campden.

"Of course you will!" I'm still unsure if this was a deceit but I gave them the benefit of the doubt… and of my acquired wisdom: Set off early; don't stop for lunch until you've gone more than half your planned distance for the day; don't, whatever you do, carry on walking without treating blisters; go through your rucksack slinging out anything you don't really need … umbrella, tank top, laptop etc. To all my advice, the men nodded and interjected 'rights', 'OKs' and 'got-yas'. Their pace was uncomfortably slow, no doubt for them as well as me, and before long, I wished them well and strode off ahead. A couple of moments later, I glanced behind me: they were out of sight and I never saw them again.

I was making such little net headway that I decided to turn off the delightful but indirect Cotswold Way and cut to the west, along a less convoluted route heading for the River Severn and the road to Gloucester. I had a good reason for wanting to forge ahead: my girls were even then on their way over from Surrey to stay with my father at his Cheltenham home. If I could get within range of the spa town, my wife had agreed to collect me, take me to Cheltenham and then return me to the same spot the next morning.

I phoned in from a place called Whitminster, no more than a hamlet on the A38 and my wife duly came by. It felt strange to go in a car again, even though it was less than a fortnight since I had parked up by Victoria coach station.

As we drove north there was plenty of news to catch up upon, but what I remember from that ride, more than anything else in my briefing on current and domestic affairs, was the sheer speed at which

CHAPTER 3: THE MENDIPS – THE MALVERNS

Above Wotton-under-Edge, looking south west over Somerset and the Severn Valley to South Wales.

Approaching Worcester.

the hedgerows seemed to be rushing by. My wife is not a particularly reckless speedster behind the wheel, but the metric plod, plod, plod of my walk through the West Country had evidently impressed itself into my psyche. After only a few hundred thousand steps, this drive felt like boldly going star trekking at warp factor nine!

We docked in Cheltenham and my children mobbed me. Isabella ran her fingers over my bristly scalp and emergent moustache. All was well.

We returned the next day to Whitminster, making sure that we had found the exact spot I had reached and I set off, soon afterwards, up the road, at high speed (for walking). There was again more than one reason for my accelerated rate of progress that day. The main one was that, planning to return that evening to a warm bed in Cheltenham, I could afford to leave my heavy load behind. Instead, I scooted along carrying only a daysack containing no more than a pack of sandwiches and my waterproof, which I had included because the weather was turning. I could well imagine how ancient people might have interpreted the elements that day; perhaps the sun-god had upset the gods of rain by boasting so heartily for so many days. Stormy vengeance was nigh, for now it was celestial payback time! The gathering cloud and the freshness in the air constituted another reason for my quick step. I reflected that, in spite of some mist on Dartmoor and a minute or two of drizzle near Redruth, I had not, until then, had call to reach for the waterproof.

Summer raindrops, as you know, can be warmer and also much bigger than wintry rain. The first few are pleasant but, if you get caught, you can be drenched in seconds. Watching the sky turn greener by degrees, I trotted into Gloucester. Near the centre of town, in the shadow of the cathedral, where Tudor buildings lean against one another, it started. I nipped into the first open door. By great good fortune, it was a tavern.

Twenty or thirty shoppers joined my dash for cover. In this part of

CHAPTER 3: THE MENDIPS – THE MALVERNS

middle England the refugees from the torrent outside seemed happy to queue up and pay the price of keeping dry. I remember thinking these people all knew that 'the decent thing' is to buy a drink, if you want to wait in a pub. The landlord didn't seem too bothered, though, as something more pressing even than a throng of shoppers at the bar, had caught his attention ... a steady drip, drip, drip from the ceiling, not too far from the electric light!

In the time of Noah (I seem to remember having been told) it rained for forty days non-stop. In Gloucester the rain came down hard for thirty-nine days, twenty-three hours and fifty minutes less than that. It was just as well that we didn't have the full measure, as at that rate anyone without an ark to hand would surely have perished. As it was, during those few minutes, enough water had fallen that the ullage bucket, more usually filled with beer, 'pulled through' at barrel changes, which had been positioned to catch the drips, had at least half-filled with rainwater!

I finished my pint as the skies cleared and stepped out onto the steaming pavement. Dazzlingly bright, the sun reflected on the shiny streets and a couple of large rats scuttled past me, no doubt seeking higher and drier hiding holes.

I passed an elegant coffee shop, where there was another queue, in spite of the fact that it had stopped raining. 'Middle England' this may have been, but a quick check on my map confirmed what I already knew: it wasn't Central England yet. Onwards, I told myself, or I'll never get there. I consciously lengthened my stride a little bit and marched northward at a speed which fitted my mumbled chanting:

"Dr Foster went to Gloucester in a shower of rain.

He stepped in a puddle, right up to his middle and never went there again!"

To the north of the city, I cut across playing fields. I passed some cricketers peering out of a pavilion at their waterlogged wicket. I had done likewise on many occasions after 'rain stops play' and

I understand why keen players are reluctant to admit defeat to the weather but, that day the wet had come in biblical volumes. Perhaps they were better judges of matters than me, but, for the life of me, I couldn't see that they had any prospect of further play that day, and wondered why they hadn't packed up and returned to their families.

My own family were touring around the Gloucestershire countryside and spotted me heading along a road south of Tewkesbury. I felt the same uplifting of spirit that I'd sensed at Wotton the day before, only this time I had the additional pleasure of a change of shirt!

You may have guessed that I am a big fan of Ian Botham, mostly because of his prowess at the wicket but also because of his 'Groats – End' walking. I would certainly not wish to belittle his efforts, but I do confess to imagining what relative comfort might be enjoyed if, like Mr Botham, one had a vanload of clean socks and shirts following along behind. Still, it was my choice to 'go it alone' and even if walking solo and carrying a pack involved greater discomfort at times, I wouldn't have had it any other way. But for the moment, I enjoyed the luxury!

There was another cloudburst in Tewkesbury. I made another dash for another pub, The Bell Hotel, there meeting a fellow who claimed to be a TV producer. He spoke for the entire duration of the storm on the subject of his next documentary, about a double agent in the war. It seemed plausible. When the rains abated I trotted across town to make the rendezvous with my girls.

"Do you know the Old Bear?" I asked a cabby.

"Was that the White Bear or the Black Bear?" he returned.

"The Old Bear," I affirmed, and got directions to both.

At the Olde Black Bear I did indeed meet the family. We had a good meal in congenial surroundings. To my knowledge, this is the only traditional-style real ale pub in Gloucestershire to be run by a Frenchman. Actually, I can't think of any other such establishment in any other county. On reflection it is not so odd – after all, the

CHAPTER 3: THE MENDIPS – THE MALVERNS

French are dedicated to food and drink, and generally make excellent hosts, yet somehow the town or country pub seems especially British. Monsieur Borgoise made friendly, unintrusive conversation.

"I will geev yer u fievair," he offered, rolling a note off a substantial wad which he pulled from his trouser pocket.

"Merçi beaucoup, monsieur" was the best I could manage after two near drownings, at least three pints, a very large meal and about twenty-two miles walked that afternoon.

Tewkesbury is an ancient market town. The abbey is Norman, consecrated in 1121, and its tower is probably the biggest and certainly one of the most intact examples from that period. The town grew up around it and along the waterside, for here the Severn and the Avon flow side by side. I had already met both of these great rivers and I knew that if I kept on schedule, I would bridge most of Britain's major watercourses in the next month.

There is a signposted footpath called the Severn Way, which meanders alongside, or near to, the river for many miles. Near centres of population, the path is well-trodden but less well maintained out of town. More than once I followed what seemed to be the main trail across fields up 'dead ends', to where cattle take water, or fisherfolk set up, and had to double-back. After one such loop, I came across a man walking in the opposite direction. He asked if I was making for Upton, which I was:

"You'd better put your long trousers on – them stingers are savage!"

I thanked him for his counsel and, remembering how Henry had chucked out my joggers, I continued – thinking that I would probably manage to fight any big ones off with a stick … Besides which, it was far too hot to contemplate putting on extra clothing.

I crossed underneath the M50 and stamped down a few stingers. So far, so good. Marching north along the path I covered another two or three miles relatively unscathed, until I came to a wild bit, which ran through shrubs, very close to the riverbank. There was absolutely no way around and the path was engulfed by head-high nettles. Scything madly, I made very slow and painful progress through the jungle. No parakeets or spider monkeys here, but undoubtedly the finest stingers in the land and also a wondrous abundance of butterflies, mostly blues and tortoiseshell – the latter helped me to ignore what was happening to my legs and arms. A few stings, children learn at an early age, are uncomfortable but soon pass. I had, by the time I escaped over a stile into the next field, been stung many hundreds, if not thousands of times, wherever there was bare skin; I was even stung through my shorts and shirt but, on each leg, the exposed skin between ankle and thigh was a fiery and puffy pink rash.

Stinging nettles are not indigenous to the British Isles – they were brought here by the Romans and planted along the roadsides for the express purpose of central heating for legionnaires who would flagellate themselves with leaf stalks – so I understand. For some reason, I remembered the bizarre 'endurance' undergone by Japanese TV game show contestants, exposed on our screens by Clive James[21]. With quivering lips, they were filmed murmuring, to diffuse the pain inflicted by various tortures. With stinging flesh, I hummed and murmured too but, unlike the Romans, who were stimulated to march more miles, my malady made me make for the first shady place I came across when I emerged in Upton-upon-Severn.

At Upton I took stock. Studying my maps and my progress I reasoned that I was slowly but surely grinding to a halt. By that stage I had already developed a kind of throbbing which went beyond the left, right, left, right rhythm of the feet. The Cotswold scenery through which I had been wandering is quite a knockout, especially in high summer. I was enjoying myself (in spite of the nettles) but I was not very much nearer John o' Groats at that time than I had been for the

---

[21] Clive James is an Australian-born author and broadcaster well-known for his wit and enjoyment of child-like humour.

last couple of days. There are picturesque rolling hills whichever way you look. There are pubs aplenty in charming sandstone villages, and I sensed that it was in those parts, and not Cornwall (as in my pupil's sceptical prediction) that I was in danger of capitulating. So I pinched myself (metaphorically rather than on my sore legs) and resolved to get a move on. I hardly took a second look at the festive streets or the town's famous bridge, and, still humming through gritted teeth, I marched doggedly down the long road joining Upton with the Malvern Hills.

CHAPTER 4

The Malverns – Stafford

IN WHICH
...I narrowly escape an untimely burial and contemplate 'Englishness'. There are a few more close encounters and lucky escapes as I make gentle progress through the Midlands. I surprise myself, yield to temptation, and eventually fall victim to a practical joke.

I met a very large number of agricultural vehicles coming towards me along that road. At some point, though I have to say not immediately, I realised the reason. Could it have been that all the farmers in the area were getting together for a tea party? In a sense, the answer was "Yes", at the Three Counties Showground, which I passed, at around 'kicking-out time'.

Among the clues I had failed to spot were the RAC signs which direct all manner of agricultural exhibitors from Herefordshire, Worcestershire and Gloucestershire, and the thousands of visitors, and also a huge cloud of dust mushrooming up into the fresh, clean air above Little Malvern, from where there are magnificent views over Gloucestershire and Worcestershire.

Walking the very length of the country gives you a feeling that you know and understand things about it which are difficult to put into words, but one phrase which came into my head in the evening sunshine was "This is England". Very perceptive of me? I don't know, but I can say that if ever you have to show an alien visitor 'Merry England', of all the places I visited on my linear route, that would probably be the best spot. Perhaps the Cornish fisherman or Cumbrian sheep farmer – maybe even suburban man, stuck in his commuter rut

CHAPTER 4: THE MALVERNS – STAFFORD

– would disagree, but what I could see seemed to encapsulate so much of what makes England England: a predominantly rural landscape with its patchwork of fields. It was easy to pick out the course of the Severn and some of the settlements in its valley. Villages linked by minor roads, church spires, oak trees, and so on. Below me and to the north, the roofs of Great Malvern were bathed in golden red.

I checked into the youth hostel and after a cool shower trained onto my sore legs, set off again, without rucksack, to take another look at the view. In an unusual pub which is part spaghetti house I spent an enjoyable evening in the company of a fellow hosteller who had travelled from the North-East for a mountain biker's rally and whose sunburn matched my nettle-rash.

Down from the youth hostel in Great Malvern, having taken in the Norman abbey and a good number of bookshops, I found a cobbler to examine my right boot, which had gone lumpy. I bought a big map of Northern England to encourage me and photocopied, onto DayGlo green, the sign for my rucksack which that scantily clad motorist in Somerset had suggested. It was a good idea. I had used my dad's computer to print out this simple message:

> LAND'S END TO
> JOHN O' GROATS
> FOR
> THE IMPERIAL CANCER
> RESEARCH FUND

It was successful, inasmuch as people reading the notice tooted, waved or gave thumbs-up, it provoked comments of general encouragement, and at other times people would stop me to press a coin into my sweaty palm. I thought of the chaps whom I'd met down by St Michael's Mount – they told me it would be a good idea to raise my profile! Another thing crossed my mind: if I needed a further statement of intent, pinning the sign felt like nailing colours to the mast. Anyone finding me in a crumpled heap by the roadside somewhere in Worcestershire would, at the very least, now know at a glance by how much I had failed, and I had cause to remind myself that I was less than a quarter of the way there!

The administration in Malvern that morning hadn't held me up for long and I was on the outskirts of Worcester by mid-morning. My first view of the cathedral came from well above the city centre where a demolished row of houses on one side of the road had made way for allotments. Through a delicate curtain of sweet peas I saw Worcester's distinctive spires and a little nearer, the county cricket ground, which looked in splendid condition. Even if there had been play I don't suppose I would have stayed for long as I was feeling strong, and I knew I had a chance of moving on to a completely new phase of the walk that day.

Ever since I had started planning, I knew that I had to go in small steps, so to speak. At Stourport, now only about fifteen miles away, I intended to pick up the Staffordshire and Worcester Canal and follow it (and other waterways) right through the Midlands. It promised to be gentle and attractive walking, and getting to the canals at Stourport was certainly my immediate goal.

My maps showed that it is possible to follow the Severn right out of Worcester – it looked a simple matter to follow the Severn Way (I braced myself for more nettles) as far as Stourport, but I managed to make a hash of it. I negotiated the first couple of miles through riverside parkland in relaxed fashion in the company of dog walkers, roller skaters and the like, but then, carelessly, lost the trail by trying to cut out what seemed to be a meander. I followed a lady and her daughter along a good path which I felt sure would meet the river again before long. It didn't. Instead we climbed a steep hill into a residential area. My pace was fractionally faster than theirs and it took a few minutes for me to overtake them and open up a bit of a gap.

"Mummy that man's walking all the way to Scotland," I heard.

CHAPTER 4: THE MALVERNS – STAFFORD

"Don't be silly," came the gruff reply.

It took me some while to track down the river again but, when I did, there were no more strollers or kids on bikes; instead there were rather a lot of cows and some, to my relief, avoidable stinging nettles.

Cows don't follow paths, they make them. Frustratingly, I followed cow tracks several times to watering places when the Severn Way headed inconspicuously in a different direction. I suppose that in my mind was the recent mistake I had made by veering away from the course of the river. If I hugged it closely then I couldn't go wrong, could I? Well, so I thought at any rate. In the end I made more meanders than the river, by some margin, but came to a rather smart-looking pub-cum-riverside restaurant. It occurred to me that there may have been some kind of altercation between the farmer and the publican, as the path which led through the pub garden came to a halt by a stile into the field which had been comprehensively barbed-wired up. There was a strongly worded sign to dissuade, I presumed, glass- and crisp-packet carrying punters straying into the meadow. Scratching my newly restored beard I remembered the Cornish farmer, with his gun, and eventually decided against vaulting the barbs and U-turned out of the pub driveway, picking up a minor road to the village of Holt.

There was a terrific commotion where the road came out at Holt Heath. A police motorcade, outriders and all, was clearing the road and forcing people to pull over.

I had thoughts of royalty, nuclear warheads and the prime minister before catching sight of an extremely slow-moving vehicle of the type which is known in the construction industry as a "muck away" lorry. It was brimful of earth and listing at a horrible angle, in my direction, not because it had a flat tyre, but because the back axle had snapped and it had completely lost its double rear nearside wheels. I pressed myself as far as I could into the hedgerow and, as it was passing, grinding and wheezing, I recalled in a moment of pessimism, having asked Henry, my Dartmoor guide, what was the worst thing which could happen to me. Being buried alive hadn't featured then but, for a long moment, it seemed on the cards now, especially bearing in mind the hand I had been dealing myself of late. Needless to say, the load passed me by and I was able to head on to Stourport along minor roads, without further incident.

Carnival bunting adorned Stourport's colourful streets. There was a funfair near the marina and a lot of people were out enjoying the sights and the sounds. To my eye, the many hanging baskets and brightly painted narrow boats, with their bucket gardens, had more appeal than had the waltzer or the ghost train. Besides which, I reasoned there would definitely not have been room for me and my rucksack in a bumper car! I had a short rest in a pub by the river before walking up the streets to the slightly higher level from which leaves the Staffordshire and Worcester Canal. There is an ingenious navigation which links the waterways. I looked over my shoulder for the last time at the Severn, snaking its way to the sea, and was struck by a kind of geographical realisation similar to when I had stood on the motorway bridge watching the M5 leading 'to the West Country'. It was as if a chapter had come to an end and ahead lay new prospects and new challenges.

Excluding diversions, I had carried my pack about twenty-six miles already that day, and it was a measure of my growing stamina and strength that I could press on without too much bother the four or five more miles along the canal to Kidderminster. Canal boats don't generally go all that much faster than I could walk – and of course, they stop at locks. Some children aboard a holiday boat spied me and were egging on their cap'n to race me.

"Faster, Daddy, he's getting away!"

I almost gave them a run for their money but had neither energy nor sustained interest in the contest. Instead I plodded on at a gentle pace enjoying the dragonflies, birdsong and on occasional plop from small fry flipping in the dark water.

CHAPTER 4: THE MALVERNS – STAFFORD

It is certainly easier to find one's way through Kidderminster on the canal than by road and a good deal more direct! I expect we all have knowledge of dire one-way systems, but Kidderminster would be in my top three, alongside Maidstone and Hemel Hempstead.

I was glad on this occasion not to be behind the wheel. It was fifteen days since I had parked in Victoria and, in the years since I passed my driving test, the longest period I could remember when I hadn't driven anywhere. Is that another reflection on modern life?

On the canals I often saw the backs of places, old buildings and factories, many of them derelict and assuredly belonging to a different age. There is even a hypnotic sense in which pacing rhythmically along these forgotten backwaters makes it easy to let the imagination drift. I suppose it's one of the reasons that winding down canal holidays are so popular. The slow pace lets you turn back the clock.

My slow pace was getting slower and slower and I came to a complete standstill where the canal passes St George's church. I looked around, thinking that I could go no further, wondering where I could stay. There were no handy fields just there, the demolition site by the towpath looked a bit ratty, and I didn't fancy the graveyard! I took out my maps and spotted a camping and caravan site by the canal at Wolverley, about two miles to the north. North was the direction I was headed, I told myself but, even so, getting going again was pretty gritty and at that stage, two miles was a marathon in itself.

I passed a pub The Lock, where evening recreational drinkers sitting outside told me not only how to get to the campsite, but also a quick way in through the back gate. "That'll save you a few yards," someone said: that's how weary I must have looked!

A fellow reading the papers, cross-legged in a deckchair outside the spacious awning of his luxury caravan, offered to help me pitch tent. He was sympathetic and not in the least patronising, and his interest and enthusiasm alone were enough to revive my drooping spirits. He came from Argyll and was touring England with his family, but enjoyed long-distance walking. Did I know the Southern Upland Way? Had I come along the Cotswold Way? How long had I been walking? Hadn't I done well?

The tent was soon ready and as I threw my rucksack inside, I overbalanced, falling forward through the zip-up door. My face landed in the padded foam lumbar supporting bands of the pack and, like a fairy tale character, I think I really did fall asleep at the moment my head hit the pillow.

I didn't sleep for long, waking around half past ten with a raging thirst. Somehow I passed by the drinking water supply tap near the back gate, through which I exited and trotted down the lane to the pub. The same people were still sitting outside. I bought a drink and had a bizarre three-way conversation between the landlord's wife, who surreptitiously organised a whip-round for me, and a rather earnest media man who wanted me to appear in a Land Rover advert!

After a generous drinking-up time I had to climb the campsite perimeter fence because the gate had been locked. I don't think that I disturbed anybody, although the mad dog which went truly berserk as I tiptoed past his owner's tent must have woken hundreds!

I made my checks in the morning: feet, head, kit. All seemed okay and I was back on the towpath before seven o'clock, which was after most of the fishermen were in place. There are thousands of their kind around Birmingham and they fill up the bank at intervals of about twenty paces. It may be that they have allotted places or else, by regular occupation, the fishermen claim right of possession. I guess that what happens follows the adage 'the early bird catches the worm'; perhaps that is why they look so sleepy and don't talk to each other, I wondered.

The fishermen no longer cast, it seems. Instead, they reach directly to the opposite bank with telescopic, carbon fibre rods of a type which I had not seen. They are held horizontal with the shorter, counterbalancing end protruding back over the towpath at around shin height. Everyone seemed to have at least one and I couldn't help

CHAPTER 4: THE MALVERNS – STAFFORD

thinking that anyone wishing to add to his portfolio of shares might do a lot worse than to find out who makes this equipment and, if it is not too late, to 'get in' on what must be big business at the dawn of our leisure age.

I returned to my dreamlike state and paced on, as the morning became hotter. I had discovered that on the Staffordshire and Worcester Canal there are more pubs per mile than on any other British waterway … and counting them was one way to assess my progress. Another possibly more systematic method was to count off the bridges, which are numbered. By noon, I had walked some sixteen miles and reached bridge number 56 (The Lock at Wolverley is by bridge 20) and I was ready for lunch, so I stopped at the next pub, The Mermaid. Roast beef, Yorkshire pudding, potatoes, two veg and a pint, all for not very much, served me fine and I was back on the trail before most people had arrived for their pre-lunch drinks. "Coming through!" is the battle cry of towpath cyclists in those parts. I discovered that, on hearing this warning, you sidestep to let the riders, usually in pairs, through… but that you do so towards the water. It means that the cyclists can pass without danger of wobbling in. The manoeuvre may not be in the Highway Code but it is certainly the way things are done – usually. The towpath at Ounsdale runs along the west bank of the canal: thus the water was on my right.

It must have been that one such call of "Coming through" was lost beneath the chug of a narrow boat's engine, because the first I knew of the cyclist was a rather desperate "Look out!" I jumped as quickly as my heavy pack would let me – to my left. This was not good news for the third party, who also had swerved left. He jerked the handlebars, bounced off my rolled-up sleeping mat and careered off over the thin strip of grass between path and water. I observed the look of horror on his face as he half-fell and half-jumped off, managing somehow to save his bike and stay dry, but it was a very close call indeed.

We both apologised. I said that it was a good job that only his words had been drowned. I was fine, he was unhurt but I didn't see him again, so I presumed he had taken a circular route – he was a *cyclist*, after all.

After all the excitement I felt the need to answer the call of nature and stopped at another pub about half a mile further on. Not wishing to offend the landlord, I bought a drink from the bar. This pub was doing a roaring trade in Sunday lunches and I could quite see why, when an extremely pretty waitress with long legs came past carrying, at about nose height, two huge helpings of steaming fare, beautifully presented.

"That looks nice," I blurted out as she came past. To my surprise she stopped and with a soft smile verging on the coquettish she asked if I had meant the food. In a flash I had decided to order some for myself. This felt almost sinful, not only because it would be my second roast beef dinner that lunchtime, but also because nobody else knew and I did nothing to disabuse them. I didn't even bother justifying to myself that I was burning off masses of energy and so needed stoking up – I just sat there and enjoyed every morsel.

There were more cyclists that afternoon. I kept my ears open and sidestepped right, which met with approval, and pleasantries were uttered in 'Brum'.[22] For my part, the cyclists caused a good deal less annoyance than they evidently caused the fishermen. When bikes 'came through' the fishermen had to lift their rods. As the barriers came up, I, too, could get through, if the timing was right and I was following a biker closely. It felt like getting out of the car park without paying. In fairness, all but the most stubborn fishermen raised their rods, and it was definitely easier for me to step over unraised rods than for the cyclists to dismount and lift their bikes across, as I saw a number of times.

---

[22] 'Brum' or 'Brummie' is the accent and dialect of Birmingham. The term is derived from Bromwichham, which is a historical variation of Birmingham.

CHAPTER 4: THE MALVERNS – STAFFORD

Restful tow path in the West Midlands.

The afternoon wore on, hot and bright, but I made good progress through surprisingly green country, wandering around Wolverhampton and roving through Featherstone.

Surprised by how easily I had skirted Birmingham, I was west of Cannock and approaching the town of Penkridge when I was bitten by a large black dog, who was running off the lead. In the distance, his owner was shouting "Drop!" to the animal, I think. He had me by the left arm but by an extraordinary piece of luck had bitten into my watch rather than into my flesh. Wasn't Peter Pan protected in a similarly charmed fashion?

The dog did drop me and, although the watch was damaged, I had only a graze. Like the bump with the bike, the biting had happened quickly. In hindsight, I probably should have made a fuss but I was feeling philosophical – it could have been worse. Besides which, dog and owner, a tall, dark figure with a Neanderthal loping stride, disappeared down another path before I had a chance to collect my wits. Furthermore, whatever pain I had in that upper limb was nothing in comparison with what I was feeling lower down. Although the canal towpaths are flat, they are knobbly and my feet were very tender. Perhaps it was that I had slightly overdone it the previous day – or perhaps my boots were wearing thin.

Even though there was nowhere obvious to camp, I fixed on the idea of staying in Penkridge. I walked through the town looking for inspiration, or possibly a bed and breakfast. There was one hotel, which was closed, and three pubs near the railway station from where people commute into Birmingham.

At The White Hart, an old coaching house, someone looked away from the big screen video long enough to tell me there was nowhere to stay. Opposite, in the Littleton Arms, the bar manager suggested that I tried Stafford, only another six miles north, and this I found very disheartening, so my last chance was the Railway Inn. As I edged

CHAPTER 4: THE MALVERNS – STAFFORD

sideways through the narrow saloon door, a well-oiled local broke into song:

"Hi ho, hi ho, it's off to work we go." He was joined, in the joke, by other drinkers. I smiled broadly which seemed the best thing to do and dumped my rucksack in the corner.

Things did not start well. In the first instance, the landlord refused to serve me. I was rather baffled, but assumed for some reason he had taken exception to my appearance, which I must admit may have been disconcerting, hairy legs, knobbly knees and a haircut from Pentonville.[23] I must have looked like trouble, or perhaps, like the canoodling couple in West Harptree, he thought I looked like a New Age traveller. Then a fellow with the physique of a professional darts player sidled up to me, downed the last inch of his lager and lifted up his glass near my face. I was on the point of making a hasty exit when he grabbed my arm.

"I'll get that, Geoff. What are you having, mate? And put one in there." He passed his mug over the pumps to the publican.

Pleased still to have my teeth, I mumbled some words of thanks and drank up. It was a few minutes later, before I'd quite finished my pint, when I began to realise what was going on. Someone else bought me another, and explained:

"Your money's no good in here."

I think they must have seen me passing the window earlier looking around and presumably something had been said since everyone had conspired in the original wind-up. I had felt sure that I was going to be duffed up; they all thought this was funny and now wanted to buy me a drink.

At some point, with about six "helpers", I erected the tent in the pub garden. It took about six times longer than normal.

---

[23] Opened in 1816, HM Prison Pentonville houses Category B and C male prisoners.

Back in the bar, I was warned about 'toffee-nosed' attitudes further into Staffordshire and informed that the best lads came from West Bromwich. Once I had become accustomed, a little more, to the deadpan accent with falling inclinations, for example:

"We all think that what you're doing is great," delivered in the same way that you might break news of bereavement or a fortune lost, I realised that these folk were warm-hearted, generous and perfectly genuine ... even if their sense of humour seemed sharp at first.

Forget raw eggs and 'grandfather's secret recipe', what you need for a hangover is a good brisk walk first thing in the morning. About six miles does it, so I marched into the historic county town bright-eyed and bushy-tailed.

CHAPTER 5

Stafford – Marple

IN WHICH
...I have a lucky break and there are more interesting encounters but, as the challenge of the Pennine Chain looms large, I suffer a serious setback.

Stafford boasts one of the largest Tudor timber-framed buildings in the country, the Ancient High House, which now accommodates the Tourist Information office (from where I bought some postcards) and many other fine old buildings, including St Chad's (Norman) Church in the High Street and the collegiate church of St Mary's. If you are in need of spiritual refreshment of a different kind, I recommend The Swan or The Vine. What I needed then, more than anything, was some breakfast. This turned out to be Cornish pasty and chips consumed on a bench in the town square. An old boy sat down next to me. He didn't say much, but accepted my offer of a chip and we sat in the sunshine, watching the world go by, each with our own thoughts. I began to overheat and remember feeling restless. I had a strong urge, not merely to get on with it (for I often felt that) but actually to walk, in spite of sore feet. I cannot explain these feelings but I understood then and there how it is that some people become physically addicted to 'pumping iron' in the gym. It was an important moment for me because I realised that my body was adjusting to the new regime. Whereas halfway through Cornwall it had been the mind ordering a dissenting body, "Come on, feet, walk!", in Stafford, one might say, the boot seemed to be on the other foot, so I didn't linger, loaded up and resumed my challenge.

A few miles to the north, on the road to Stone, I was intercepted by a talkative Welshman, who walked with me, for a while, as far as Yarlet Hall prep school, where he worked as groundsman. He reminisced about the day when Ian Botham had come past that very spot, with his entourage on *his* marathon walk, in the other direction. I had a full tour of the grounds and remember feeling mildly curious whilst making comparisons between the facilities of that school of those of my own. For a while, we watched some French students on summer camp playing rounders, and there were various introductions, amongst which I recall a perspiring and bare-chested lad who was vigorously forking a rose bed, under the baking sun… and also a cuddly cook who promised my guide that she had saved him a piece of his favourite pie. I have heard it said that prep school communities are sheltered and, particularly if you 'live in', it is possible to exist in a way which distances you from the big, wide world outside. In acute cases, you go potty, or walk from Land's End to John o' Groats. I felt relaxed and somewhat privileged to have been admitted into their world at Yarlet Hall… but my mind was firmly fixed on the wide world outside. I knew that the Pennines were just a couple of days ahead of me and I was itching to hit the hills and feel the wind in my stubble. I thanked them and slipped away.

It was late afternoon and I had been dreamily canal walking for a while near Stone when I next made contact with the real world. A couple of men were sitting outside a pub drinking. Nothing odd about that, you may think but, as I approached, a funny thought came across me and I grinned.

"What's so funny?" one of them asked. There was no aggression in his tone but I sensed a potentially embarrassing situation.

I explained what had tickled me:

"Well, there you two are, taking it easy…" (they did look sublimely relaxed with beer glasses and sunglasses) "…and here's me toiling along with this pack. I just wondered what on earth I was doing."

"What on earth are you doing?"

CHAPTER 5: STAFFORD – MARPLE

And so I sat down with them to explain.

They reassured me of the worth of my trek by contributing to the sponsorship fund, and easily persuaded me to accept a drink. We sat on patio chairs on the terrace, like men do, cross-legged with foot on knee (probably with hands behind the head) and spoke of people and places. These men worked in Penkridge at the Agricultural College near The Railway Inn where I had set out from that same day, but were coming to terms with the start of their long summer holidays. They gave me some local advice about the course of the canal and confirmed that my idea of staying at Trentham Park, some six miles further, was a good one, as there was a fully equipped campsite at that place.

Trentham Park is enormous. The buildings of Trentham Hall are in disrepair, but the expansive grounds are running as a successful business. So far as the camping goes, the site is better suited to car drivers pulling caravans than to solo long-distance walkers, as even to enter the place is a long haul, along and around confusing driveways. When, finally, I reached the security barriers, I was handed a fistful of leaflets about the many activities on offer. To be honest, I didn't really give them more than a second glance, but I believe they included information about waterski jumping, cyclo-cross and the like. All I wanted was to pull my boots off and contemplate my navel.

I pitched my tent on gently undulating land within streaking distance of the shower block and after an indulgent half-hour, or so, in that building, I stepped out into the long shadows which were falling across the grass. I felt refreshed and invigorated, and presumably my cheeks had a rosy glow to match the sinking sun.

Having decided to explore the gardens, I wandered around for a while. Bats were swooping around the buildings. I like bats, for I understand that each one can consume up to two hundred mosquitoes per hour. I mused that in spite of the bats, there would always be more mosquitoes, so it didn't matter anyway. I was still being philosophical as I reassured myself of my own policy relating to insects and my tent (which had an integral mosquito net): there is no admittance to any flying creature. The only crawling creature admitted is me. Any infringement is punishable by death. Executions to be carried out by crushing.

Murderous thoughts left me as I came across the extensive and well maintained Italianate gardens. The sun had been down for, I suppose, an hour. I recognised some of the fragrances, tobacco plants, jasmine and honeysuckle ... It was all rather pleasant, the more so because I was completely alone. I flattered myself that all these flowers were blooming for me.

Beyond a hotel and conference centre (within the grounds) I spotted an attractive pub and headed that way. Inside, a slick DJ was mixing quiz questions with record requests. I was drawn into the whole affair and caught myself racking my brain to recall the name of Peters and Lee's chart-topping hit of 1973.[24]

Someone came around selling raffle tickets and it turned out that I had the lucky winning ticket. My prize was to come forward to play their version of 'Strike It lucky' which, I understand, is a TV game show. You have to answer questions.

"We have a winner. What's your name?" asked the DJ.

"Jonathan." That was easy enough, I thought.

"This is John." (That always ever so slightly annoys me.) "Where are you from, John?" That was a little bit harder – I considered saying "Land's End" but didn't.

"So are you on holiday, or just passing through?"

"Just coming through."

The questions did get a bit harder, but I didn't give any wrong answers and, soon enough, I was asked if I was ready for the final question, for the big cash prize! Would I "strike it lucky"? Well, there

---

[24] "Welcome Home" was originally a French song which the successful pop and folk duo Lennie Peters and Dianne Lee recorded after winning the TV talent show *Opportunity Knocks*.

CHAPTER 5: STAFFORD – MARPLE

was certainly an element of luck because the jackpot question was about snakes indigenous to Britain. All I had to do was name two and, since I had seen a few grass snakes that week and nearly trod on that adder on Bodmin Moor, I had good reason to be confident of my answer. Everyone cheered and, rather better off than I had been at any time since Cornwall, I trotted back to the campsite.

At first light I did some serious thinking: my maps showed that I could reach the Peak District National Park quite comfortably that day. From there, I could climb onto the High Peak and pick up the start of the Pennine Way at the Derbyshire village of Edale. All of that seemed very exciting, but there were attractive alternatives which would steer me north of the notoriously boggy first miles of the Pennine Way. In the end, I surprised myself and stuck with my original planning and headed north towards Kidsgrove.

If ever you are in Newcastle-under-Lyme, by the way, do stop for breakfast at Oaties on the A34. They specialise in traditional oatcakes, which they cook before your eyes and load up with bacon and eggs, or anything else you want. It was so delicious that once I'd finished mine, I queued up again with the lorry drivers for a packed lunch!

I joined the Macclesfield Canal at Kidsgrove. It is not as busy as some of the other waterways I had followed up to that point. Parts of it are very narrow indeed and there are wider passing places. The canal itself is part of the so-called "Ring" which links six historic canals to form a circular route around the county of Cheshire. There were more dragonflies and fisherfolk, although fewer of the former than in Somerset, and far fewer of the latter than in Warwickshire. Of recreational cyclists there were several pairs which 'came through', as I paced the towpath towards Congleton.

For a little bit of variety, in mid-afternoon, I left the canal where its course was less than direct, and climbed up to a little road bridge.

A young man was sitting on the wall with a can of Coke. He got up and started trotting along beside me. He asked me where I was going but, without waiting for a reply, proudly informed me that he had come there on the back of a tractor. He explained that he attended a special school nearby. It was en route, and he offered to show me his school. We walked together for a couple of miles, during which time he spoke with great enthusiasm of the horses he knew. Sure enough, when we reached the school, the animals were there, just as he had described, grazing in the grounds. A piebald pricked up his ears and trotted over when he saw the lad. It was obvious from the mutual affection that this was 'his horse' and it was touching to see. He apologised that he had to be getting back and, after reassuring me that he was fine and showing me another two cans of drink inside his bag, he trotted off back down the hill in the direction from which we had just come.

As the sun got lower in the sky, I made for the village of Sutton Lane Ends, which is south-west of Macclesfield and where my map showed a campsite. Asking directions in The Lamb, I was immediately taken by the atmosphere within. This was more than a building in which beer was sold, it was a focal point for the community, in the traditional style. Everybody knew everybody, but they welcomed an outsider without reservation. They also knew the farmer on whose land the campsite was, so it didn't take long for me to sort out my sleeping arrangements.

I continued to enjoy the ambience (and the local brew), chatting with the villagers well into the evening. It transpired that they were preparing to bury one of their number the next morning. The deceased was a gentleman who had lived in the village for nearly ninety years. I talked with his elder brother, who was very wise. In brotherly love he spoke freely and did so without trace of sorrow or remorse. He understood what, as a young man attending my own grandfather's funeral, I had failed to comprehend when I listened to the priest speaking not of sadness, but of joy and giving thanks for a long and happy life.

CHAPTER 5: STAFFORD – MARPLE

I wanted to know about village life in days gone by. Of course there had been many changes, the old gentleman explained. I didn't doubt him, although I got the feeling that in those parts, country life must have changed a good deal less than it has in other regions. There are no drive-thru hamburger joints in Sutton Lane Ends.

Heavy rain that evening cleared the air. For some hours I lay awake in my tent, listening to the drumming on the flysheet and thinking of all sorts of things. I had been deeply struck by the sincerity of the people I had met that evening. At the same time, my own memories were sorting themselves into two categories: recent memories of events whilst walking; and distant recollections of 'pre-walk' experiences. I was exhilarated and brimming with excitement on account of my adventure. 'What next?' was the ever-present issue in my consciousness. Whatever it would be, my resolution was strong. I knew it had to be, with the Pennine Way ahead of me, but just how strong, I can honestly say, I had little idea.

I had collected an additional item of luggage at The Lamb, a tie, which they had presented to me rather late in the evening. In Macclesfield the next morning, having neither shirt with collar, nor occasion to wear one, I carefully rolled up the tie and mailed it home, together with a map or two. I looked around the town for a while, as I waited for the shops to open. My boots were wearing rather thin and I had decided to buy some lightweight fell boots, which wouldn't need much breaking in. I consumed a trucker's breakfast with ease, and visited the tourism office where a cheerful lass gave me details of the Middlewood Way. This is a 'dual carriageway footpath', if you can have that, which leads north from Macclesfield along the course of a disused railway line. One side is reserved for cyclists and walkers, while beyond a single wire, horses and riders have the run of things.

In my new soft boots, I made brisk progress along the pathway before stopping for lunch in what, at one time, was a station building, north of Bollington, but which had conveniently been converted into a pub. Therein, I chatted with a family who earlier had broken their cycle ride to contribute to my sponsorship fund. After some time, we exchanged farewells for a second time and parted in opposite directions.

It was quite a surprise when, about half an hour later, I spotted the same people coming towards me along the towpath of the canal. Of course they must have looped around or something, but it was a curious event which sticks in my mind. People have asked me if I felt lonely on a solo walk of this duration, to which I reply that I met hundreds of people en route, nearly all of whom were excellent company, but this family were among the very few I ever clapped eyes on more than once. My linear route was bringing me into contact with a succession of people in a succession of places, each meeting like a snapshot of those lives whose paths intersected with my own. In that sense, repeat meetings were incongruous, and rather nice.

I had switched back onto the Macclesfield Canal so that I could experience the famous flight of locks at Marple. Some waterway workers, who were searching for a leak in a small aqueduct over the disused railway, told me that Marple Bridge was only about five miles to the north. I knew that, even allowing for a stop, I could cover that distance in less than two hours. To my left there were views across the suburbs of Manchester. The focus of my attention was not, however, in that direction but to the north, across the canal, where the shapes of the High Peak and the Pennines, cold and grey, were looming.

Black clouds gathered as I came to the first of Marple's locks; at the third a few raindrops caused me to reach for my waterproof, and by the fourth, I was running for cover from a terrific deluge, which flooded the streets alongside in moments.

Initially, I took cover under a tree, but when it became obvious that the rain was there to stay, I opted to go into town, to consider my options. It had been my intention to spend the night at the youth hostel at Crowden, some eleven miles ahead and, from that place, to begin my assault on the Pennine Way the next morning, after a night's sleep in a bed and a good breakfast. But the heavens were telling differently, so I began to wonder if I should seek out a 'B and B' there and then – I could collect the large-scale maps which my wife had sent on to the youth hostel in the morning, couldn't I? Consolidating my position, by darting for a bus shelter, I was still in a hopeless state of indecision. Water dripped from the hood of my cagoule onto my nose, as I stared out through the weather. I did not focus my gaze but I could tell from the haze of reflected light at pavement level that the rain was rebounding back from the tarmac to a height of about six inches. For the first time, I began to feel cold and shivery. I watched some cigarette ends float away into the gutter and down a drain. In that shelter, I had surely come to an impasse. There was nowhere dry to rest the rucksack, so I slouched against the concrete upright, wearing my load, for about an hour, feeling utterly miserable.

CHAPTER 6

Marple – Huddersfield

IN WHICH
... my problems are compounded. I come face to face with a shark (in the Pennines), feel the long arm of the law, and concede defeat to the weather – but people take pity on me, and the challenge limps on.

At the first sign of abatement, I took a deep breath and marched into the town, fixed on the idea of 'checking in' to any place which would have me and where I could literally lay up for the rest of the afternoon. All the walking guidebooks I had read agreed that you should give yourself 'time off' on marathon treks, perhaps a day to rest, take stock, resupply or to do something completely different, like sightseeing or receiving psychotherapy. Broadly speaking, I had walked all day, every day, for twenty days and I reckoned that now was a good time not to be heading into wild country. Unfortunately, and to my surprise, I couldn't find anywhere that offered me any encouragement... no campsites, no 'B and Bs', no youth hostels. It was still raining hard and the people I asked were understandably reluctant to stop to rack their brains or to give long-winded directions. I remember I came across a pub called The Pineapple Inn. Feeling confident, I enquired at the bar, only to be told that all the rooms were let out to the council for the purpose of stop-gap housing.

If some people get SAD[25] in the winter months, I became entrenched with wet weather-induced SIPS (stay in pub syndrome) and munched

---

[25] Seasonal Affective Disorder (or SAD) is a form of depression experienced by many at the same time each year, most commonly at the beginning of winter.

CHAPTER 6: MARPLE – HUDDERSFIELD

a brace of Mars bars whilst studying the froth formations in my glass of creamy Manchester ale.

I was waiting for inspiration, which came to me at the arrival of a vivid rainbow, shining through the bottle glass windows of the saloon. Sure enough, the sun had come out, very bright, and within moments the rain had stopped. My afternoon in bed was not to be!

I checked the maps again. Was there an outside chance that I could make it to the youth hostel at Crowden after all? I thought probably not, but stepped out in that direction all the same. I had been lucky in the past with finding places to stay. If all else failed, there was always the option of camping 'wild' in the hills.

Judging by the number of mills in that area, along the Goyt Valley, the textile industry must have been thriving at one time, although it is not now. As I surveyed first the canal engineering and then the mills, my imagination was giving me another history lesson, which was interrupted by the onset of another deluge. The nearest cover was The Lanes End Inn, to which I scampered, along the road out of Marple Bridge. This time the storm lasted about forty minutes. In that time, having ascertained that there was no prospect of a bed there, I was interviewed by the landlord and his locals. The host himself was a motorbike enthusiast and I told him of the End to Enders Association and how you can qualify for membership, whatever your mode of transport, so long as your challenge is logged and you complete the journey. Lots of people cycle the length of Britain, others have 'End to Ended' in vintage cars, or in wheelbarrows, on roller skates and the like, but this publican was fixed on the idea of biking it with his mates. He was a man of action and made plans then and there, setting dates and gaining assurance of company from others, either present in person or on the end of one of several quick phone calls made from his mobile at the bar. He also had an Instamatic camera and, if you go in there, you might be able to see my photograph, pinned up above the bar.

It was probably around eight when I rejoined my own 'End to End' challenge. The rains had abated but there was a distinct nip in the air and I had no hesitation in zipping my fleece right up to my chin. I also made certain that my waterproof was immediately grabbable, right at the top of my rucksack. As the scenery became gradually grander, there was a sense in which the individual became increasingly insignificant and I suddenly felt rather exposed, like something out of one of those epic scenes by German Romantics, who painted vast, dark representations of nature, with tiny little people somewhere in the middle. I hummed some Mahler (for there is one such painting on the sleeve of my record of the Titan Symphony), but became concerned with matters practical, when a warning I had read sprang to mind:

'There are no more superstores until Edinburgh'.[26]

Thinking, in the circumstances, that it would be foolhardy not to stock up – and also with an eye to finding somewhere warm and dry to stay – I decided to loop back and down into the town of Glossop, from where the twinkling street lamps and coloured lights gave out a reassuring glow.

I did stock up with provisions at a convenience store on the outskirts of town. I reckoned that my bulging pack must have been as heavy as it had been at any time since Dartmoor but, then again, I was about to join what long-distance walkers call 'The Toughest Trail'.

There was no room at The George Hotel, nor place to stay in any other part of Glossop and Old Glossop, as far as I could discover, but in one pub I was given a list of phone numbers for 'B and Bs'. They had a payphone, of the type which gobbles money. It was passed to me over the bar and the flex was not long enough to take it to anywhere quiet, so I did my best, with a finger in one ear and the

---

[26] *Land's End to John o'Groats: A choice of footpaths for walking the length of Britain* (Andrew McCloy, Coronet, 1994), a truly inspirational text.

CHAPTER 6: MARPLE – HUDDERSFIELD

receiver jammed to the other. Some milliseconds into the call, the pips sounded and I was grappling with the zipper on my shorts (the pocket zip) when, sensing my distress, a woman on the next bar stool ably assisted, and with a free hand unzipped the pocket. I was able to reach inside and insert a coin, just in time to get confirmation that there were no vacancies on that number. The 'follow-on call' feature seemed to be inoperative (perhaps I pressed the wrong button) and anyway, I was out of change. I carried phone cards but had made a conscious decision not to carry lots of coinage. There is a consideration of weight but also of irritation at even a few coins jingling endlessly in the pocket. I tried to attract the barman's attention, without success. The same woman stood up and, with something of a struggle herself, reached inside her own trousers to retrieve some coins from a back pocket. She had enough for a few more unsuccessful phone calls, though not enough to change the note which I had tried to change over the bar, and she wouldn't let me negotiate to reimburse her. No doubt she had caught the drift of my predicament.

"Why don't you try The George? They'll have a room."

"No, I'm afraid they're full."

And then, without hesitation, she offered:

"Well, you can stay with us if you like."

Now I was uncertain as to what to do or say. I wondered, in particular, whether the 'us' was a plural 'us' or an 'us' in the sense of "Give us another vodka, Phil"… which was almost the next thing she said. Unlike me, the woman had no trouble in attracting the barman's attention. I was somewhat wary of being picked up by a single woman at closing time in a bar, but she had a kindly smile and my mind was made up when she pointed out her husband, who was playing pool with mates, on the other side of the bar. I stopped hedging and accepted her offer.

'Drinking-up time' was lengthy and it was really quite late by the time the last pool ball was pocketed. I was still feeling rather awkward because the cueman did not seem especially taken with the idea of me coming back to his house. He didn't say anything to convey that notion, although it seemed to me as if he struck the balls with rather too much force than was necessary. It may have been that he was just annoyed with himself for missing. I couldn't tell for sure, but the strange events which followed gave me cause to wonder.

We got into their car, which wheezed and spluttered over the road to a petrol station. It cut out in the forecourt, I think it was actually out of petrol and rolled up to a pump.

The vehicle was recharged with a quick squirt, enough, I imagined, to get us back across the road to the pub, but little further. On the way back to their house, they argued about the car. It had started to rain again and the windscreen wipers were broken. Also, I would bet that the headlights were dimmer than would satisfy an MOT test engineer.

"What do you expect from a car costing £200?" was his rhetorical answer to a cutting comment from his wife.

Their home was on an estate a couple of miles away. They had a large number of children, by other marriages, and also lots of pets. There were cats and dogs, appropriately enough, given the weather conditions, as well as rabbits, rats, goldfish and so forth… but also a shark, which swam up and down in a murky aquarium in their sitting room. I put my nose up against the tank and stared through the glass at the creature. This was no man-eater but, if fish can have expressions, his was mean. Although I thought it at the time, I didn't let on that it reminded me, strongly, of dogfish dissections at school… and, in particular, how 'double biology' on a Friday morning was inevitably followed by "fish", of what we perceived to be dubious quality, for lunch! I gave the shark a last look, excused myself and pitched tent in the front garden, in the rain, watched through the open door by two or three of the youngsters. They asked me about what I was up to, and told me stories about their pets.

CHAPTER 6: MARPLE – HUDDERSFIELD

I got some sleep, in spite of a thunderstorm and thrashing wind and rain. It was a stern test for my tent, which was partially sheltered in the shadow of the house but I was woken up by banging of a different kind. Torch-bearing police officers hammered on the front door, which was right by the head of my tent. They were investigating reports of a 'domestic disturbance'.

I listened intently and later I, too, was interviewed by the officers. There had been, for sure, some kind of rumpus going on, which subsided... as did the thunder, shortly afterwards. Now I really did feel uncomfortable, mulling over the thought that my presence might have been an aggravating factor in the dispute ... I don't know.

All was peace and calm in the morning when I was offered "a brew" and asked if I liked scrambled eggs. The woman's voice was even lower and more husky than the previous night. I nearly asked whether the Pope was Catholic, but accepted the breakfast with profuse thanks.

I was driven back into town, to a point some way along the road to Crowden. I waited until the car had lurched, backfiring, out of sight and then walked back into the centre of Old Glossop. There was no need for me to go there, other than to satisfy myself that I would cover all the ground on foot. As I saw it, either I was walking from Land's End to John o' Groats, or I wasn't. People have asked me if I was tempted to cheat, and it is true that nobody would have been the wiser had I carried on from my drop-off point – nobody, that is, except me. So I got my bearings and within a few minutes came back to the doorstep of The George. I knew that I had walked to there so, with conscience satisfied, I doubled back, aiming for the Longdendale Trail.

The Longdendale Trail is a newly constructed walkway and cycle route which heads up the valley and forms part of a Trans Pennine Trail from Southport to Hull. It is surfaced in compacted, gritty sand, which made for possibly the most comfortable underfoot conditions on my entire walk. One's feet become incredibly sensitised to surfaces in a way totally unlike when, having jumped out of the car, you step from flagstone pavement to tarmac road, maybe over a grass verge – without noticing or giving a second thought. The fact is that even in heavy boots, there is a huge variance in what I imagine must be the amount of 'give'.

There is also something in the amount of 'knobbliness' which, on a long march, may make walking over some surfaces (like Forestry Commission roads), pure agony. From my experience, the very best is spongy, dry grass, growing on peaty soil which has been nibbled short by grazing animals.

In the distance I caught sight of two figures coming towards me. They were completely shielded against the driving rain in matching waterproofs, with only their eyes peeping out. Had their suits been white and not blue they might easily have passed for radiation workers inside a contaminated power plant. They crinkled towards me. The taller figure paused and, in a muffled voice, questioned me:

"Is it you, or is it us, who are mad?" My answer seemed obvious in the circumstances.

"I suppose all three of us are!"

A double dose of misfortune lay ahead at the youth hostel. Firstly, I had arrived on the only day of the week when it was completely shut down, so I couldn't collect the maps I needed for the next fortnight. Not only this but, while I was contemplating the implications by the roadside, a juggernaut with unswerving accuracy shot a broad jet of standing water my way. The rising wave caught me full in the face and a bucket load forced under my slackened hood, drenching my body on the inside of my waterproof. It was really very skilful and must have been worth a couple of hedgehogs or bunnies.

I found a wall to cower behind as I reached for a route description of the ascent of Black Hill. The papers became drenched, too, not from the rain, which was practically horizontal and bouncing off the wall, but from water drainpiping through my sleeves and down my arms.

CHAPTER 6: MARPLE – HUDDERSFIELD

I was not completely mapless, as the Pennine Way is marked on the O.S. Travelmaster map of the whole of Northern England, which I carried for an overview. I had also the aforementioned (and wet) route description… and I had a new compass. Nevertheless, the howling wind and low cloud filled me with shivery trepidation as I took my first steps along the path.

Black Hill is not well liked by walkers. The illustrious Wainwright[27] nearly drowned there, in the bog, which extends to its 582-metre summit. I have to say that I would never wish to return there, at least in those conditions, for, though the country is wild and there are doubtless fine views over the Peak District, there was nothing to see *that* day, and my head remained down as I trudged upwards through the goo.

Occasionally, I can remember being left with no option but to come down from the hills. Once or twice in Snowdonia, for example, failing light and atrocious weather had forced my arm. In such times the only thing to do is to lose height. It is foolhardy not to do so and every year there are tragedies. I may not have been in imminent danger of death but I was extremely cold and tired. I couldn't be sure of how many hours it would take me to get to Mankinholes Youth Hostel – I guessed about eight – and the Holmfirth road, down towards the Yorkshire village of Holme, seemed a better bet, so I cut across to where there was a car park and viewpoint by the roadside. As I stepped onto the road itself, I was literally blown off my feet and fell heavily on the tarmac. When loaded, my rucksack is high and wide … it certainly offers a good deal of wind resistance, and a few metres down the road I was thrown to the ground for the second time. It took me a moment or two to get up. A motorist

---

[27] Alfred Wainwright (1907-91) was a fell walker, illustrator and author. He devised the "Coast to Coast walk" across Britain and his book *Pictorial Guide to the Lakeland Fells* is regarded as a classic reference guide for hill walkers in Cumbria.

had seen me fall and stopped, nobly winding down his window and getting a dousing, similar to my own, for his trouble. He offered me a lift. Through clenched teeth I managed a smile and waved him on, thinking, as I did so, of my words that morning with the other walkers and concluding, "Yes, I must be mad."

I rubbed my eyes in disbelief, like a cartoon character, a few minutes later, when I saw someone actually cycling *up* the steep road towards me on a fully laden touring bike, directly into the wind.

"Bravo!" I called out spontaneously, "I thought I was hard ..." He smiled and grunted through a thick, black beard. He was followed, after a moderate gap, by a second cyclist, who turned out to be a young woman, whom I also congratulated. I would not want to appear sexist, for I have known some formidably strong women, but this lady must, I thought, have been incredibly fit and strong to do what she was doing. Not only that, but from the calm, sweet smile she wore, she even appeared to be enjoying it!

The same could not be said for me as I squelched down into Holme. The soft boots I had bought in Macclesfield had been saturated for hours and some of the stitching had already given way. My teeth were chattering and my right leg was sore from the second fall, but my mood transformed when I caught sight of The Fleece with its welcoming lights and a large blackboard advertising "Hot and Cold Food served all day".

I took off everything I could, whilst remaining decent, and left the sodden garments in a pool inside the porch. I ordered a brandy and made a dart for the loo, where I spent far too long standing in front of the hand dryer repeatedly pressing the button for more hot air. When, eventually, I emerged, with steaming shorts and shirt, I ordered soup and stew, which came in no time and tasted as delicious as any meal I have ever had.

The landlord in The Fleece is a great joker and he will have you in stitches if you visit, but he is also a charity fundraiser *par excellence*.

He immediately reached into his own pocket to sponsor me and irresistibly invited his customers and staff to do likewise. I heard stories of fundraising stunts which he had engineered and he even offered me a very special shirt, worn and autographed by Brendan Foster.[28] It had been auctioned, purchased and subsequently returned on three occasions to raise more cash. The shirt was mine, if it would help, he explained, but I declined. I felt sure it would get soggy and spoilt if I took it and, besides, it seemed to belong there.

Mightily fortified by the victuals, I offered some words of thanks and after a last blast, or five, from the hand dryer, I set off again down the road north-eastwards.

Although not as hard, it was still raining lower down, so visibility was poor and my own field of vision was restricted by the blinkering effect of my hood. I contemplated the gutter and offer the following observation on the subject of wheel trims: there are thousands of these spin-offs by the side of Britain's roads. Their distribution is dependent on several factors, two of which are the terrain of the road and the number of sad collectors with trainspotting mentalities. Where, by virtue of remoteness, there are none of the latter, one gets a clearer picture of where and why they come off. There is no doubting that your hubcaps are most likely to frisbee free when braking and cornering, as people must have done on this particular snaking descent, in their hundreds. My advice to drivers would be to get the braking done before entering the corner and also not to be unduly bothered or wooed by the motor trade into replacing missing hubcaps. I am not convinced of their practical merit – apparently they may be a factor in reducing drag – but so is closing the window, and if you want to cut down on noise and petrol consumption, you

---

[28] Brendan Foster was a long-distance runner. He won gold medals at the Commonwealth Games and European Championships, and Olympic Bronze in the 10,000 metres in Montreal in 1976. He is the founder of The Great North Run.

would be better off reducing your speed by a couple of miles per hour. I could happily live without fridge magnets, plug-in air fresheners, ankle warmers or go-faster stripes, so perhaps we would all be better off without replacement wheel trims.

By mid-afternoon I had reached Holmfirth, a busy town which attracts flocks of curious tourists. They come to see where Nora Batty[29] lives and to buy souvenirs of 'Last of the Summer Wine'. I saw no TV shoots going on that day, nor could I muster any great enthusiasm for hunting down the places in which they may have been, but I did buy a postcard or two all the same.

There are lots of tea shops in Holmfirth, all with very narrow doorways and closely packed tables. For someone like me, with all my kit, the layout in these parlours is thoroughly unpractical, so I forewent the chances of picking up a toasted teacake and a bill for smashed crockery, opting instead to carry on down along the road leading to Huddersfield.

In that valley, high chimneys from more textile mills give further clues about that region's industrial past. I stopped to photograph one, which was right alongside a church tower. The chimney was by far the taller and more prominent feature, and I wondered if any inference could be taken about the relative importance of industry and religion. I was packing the camera away when I became conscious that my feet were numb. I wiggled my toes but, from the lack of sensation, I was reminded of how it is at the dentist when you are invited to rinse and then dribble antiseptic pink mouthwash down your front, through anaesthetised, unresponsive lips. I sat down on a low stone wall by the pavement (the valley was rather precipitous behind me) and unlaced my fell boots. I unrolled a sopping sock and stared in horror for what I had uncovered, being bluish-white,

---

[29] Nora Batty is the fictional battleaxe in pinnie and curlers, portrayed by British actress Kathy Staff, in the world's longest-running TV sitcom, *Last of the Summer Wine*.

very puffy, pitted and wrinkled, more closely resembled an ageing suet pudding than anything vaguely foot-like. I prodded a wrinkly bit with my penknife and nearly scraped off the outer centimetre, before recognising that what I was doing probably wasn't all that sensible. Instead, I sat there and gingerly massaged each foot in turn, through the towelling dishcloth which served as my bath towel. Gradually the numbness began to pass and in its place came waves of hot, shooting pain which receded into a dull ache, a background for the next wave of pain. Feeling sorry for myself, and concluding that it was just as well that I wasn't a woman – for I don't imagine I would have coped very well with childbirth – I continued rubbing and prodding until the bottom of my feet had changed colour, to what marketing people working for paint manufacturers would probably call 'white with a hint of peach blossom'. Deep within the cavernous compartments of my rucksack I found the closest thing I had to a pair of dry socks and eased them into active service over my swollen plates.

The fell boots were clearly no good, so I wrung them out and bagged them along with my other socks, choosing instead to try my lightweight cricket shoes which I had been carrying and wearing if I went out of the tent in the evenings. The laces had to be slackened considerably but I was able to slip them on. As I rose stiffly, lifted the pack and started up again, people returning from Holmfirth must have thought me a pretty odd sight. I walked with straight legs and a double limp in the manner of a child who has wet himself – and if anyone had cared to look, they would have seen a large damp patch on the back of my shorts, too … It was rainwater from the wet wall. In that fashion, I hobbled into Huddersfield, fixing on the idea of slumping in some dark, velour-upholstered saloon seat for an hour or two. From that position of shelter I could formulate a revised plan of action. I was a long way off my planned route and also I had little or no idea of how my 'cauliflower foot' condition would develop. Apart from that, if there was no improvement, it was curtains.

I had some cause for optimism because, moments after reaching Lockwood, which is the first built-up area of town, I came across the perfect place to use as a strategic base, The Red Lion. It was the nearest thing I had to a home just then, and I executed the slumping phase of my plan without any bother. It seemed clear that I had to lay up, or at the very least, ease up.

Another day of marching in saturated fell boots would surely earn me a lengthy stay in hospital. All my clothes were wet, as was my tent, rolled up in its bag. I was conscious, too, that my sleeping bag was unaired and I was very grateful not still to be up on Saddleworth Moor for the night. So the best thing, I reasoned, would be to try, as I had done the previous evening, to find a hotel or bed and breakfast. I sidled up to the bar.

"I'm looking for somewhere to stay. Can you suggest anywhere, please?"

There followed some considerable debate amongst those on stools at the bar about the best place for me. One place was suggested, then ruled out because 'they were too snooty' and another because it was too far, and a third because it was closed down. There was, however, a boarding house, quite nearby, which was discussed and, having met with almost unanimous agreement, was on the point of being chosen, when a voice piped up:

"...Or you could stay with me."

The voice came over to qualify his offer. He was a tall, thin man in, I guessed, his forties, and his name was Joseph Kelly. If I had hedged the previous evening at the uncertainty of being picked up from a bar by a single woman, I was probably doing the same then and there, but Joseph must have read my thoughts.

"Don't worry," he said, "I'm not like *that*!"

He explained that he lived just up the road and that he had offered because he was on his own that week. His daughter was away and, besides, he would be glad of the company.

CHAPTER 6: MARPLE – HUDDERSFIELD

At that stage, I was in two minds as to whether I should take up his offer, or try the boarding house. Either way, it seemed likely that I would have a roof over my head that night, so I was heartily relieved. Joseph did my thinking for me.

"Why pay for a hotel? You can have a hot bath and ..."

"Thank you!" I interrupted. The mention of the bath had made up my mind, so I bought him a drink and the deal was done.

My companion was very sincere and he definitely hadn't been kidding when telling me he lived just up the road. As we left the pub he nipped across the road through a gap in traffic too short for my painful steps and paced off up the steep gradient of the road opposite at a rate of knots. It was more than I could do to keep up, so I didn't try. Fortunately he waited and, very fortunately, it really wasn't far.

Inside he gestured for me to sit down. Whilst mugs of tea were made, I surveyed his sitting room. Photographs on the mantelpiece caught my eye.

There were views I recognised from the Lake District, including one from a craggy summit. A pair of hiking boots in the corner confirmed my suspicions about his hobby. That's why he made such short work of the ascent to his house! I realised that I had said nothing about what I was up to, and neither had he asked. Wondering if he could have missed seeing my rucksack, I told him that I liked walking, too. It was a gross lie. At that time I hated walking. I should have said: 'I used to like walking and I hope to enjoy it again someday.'

When he asked me how long it had taken me from Edale, I knew that he had worked out that I must have been attempting the Pennine Way. He must have worked out that I had been driven down from the hills by the bad weather. I supposed that my drowned rat impersonation had given that much away.

Joseph said that there was a good soul group playing in another pub later on and after the promised bath and a curry (which turned out to be goat) at a West Indian café, both of which I enjoyed enormously, we met up again to hear the band. Their music was both good and loud, so conversation was limited. Nevertheless, I felt happy and relaxed and remember being greatly entertained by the coolest of bass players who hammered out funky riffs, with his eyes shut, even when the lead guitar tried to give him the nod to 'make a break'… with the result that the frontman became more and more wound up as his signals were repeatedly not received. It was a funny moment and an enduring memory.

Joseph's daughter's bed was warm and comfortable. I had spread clothes and equipment over radiators around the house and in the morning everything was dry, except my boots. A foot inspection had revealed that, although there was still some puffiness, most of the fluid (which must have been filling all those layers of extra skin tissue) had dispersed. Walking was painful, but the predominant sensation was one of tingling 'pins and needles'. Talking about walks and walking, over a mug of strong coffee, restored my enthusiasm and I decided to try going gently across town in my cricket shoes. It was a decision all the easier to take, as it was a fine, dry morning.

CHAPTER 7

Huddersfield – Malham

IN WHICH
… my plans change again. I get myself back on the trail and hit Brontë territory but miss a rendezvous.

Huddersfield's heyday must have been in the 19th century, for all the main buildings, the large mill owners' houses, the churches, the railway station, the market hall and the town hall (home of a certain choral society) date from that time. Nowadays, I suspect that there are fewer jobs in textiles than there are locally in engineering or the chemical industry. As for economic prosperity, I would not be qualified to comment, although, if motor cars can be used as any kind of yardstick, I did notice plenty of nice ones on the ring road, including almost as many 'off-roaders' as there are at home in Surrey … although I couldn't help feeling that, in these parts, they had a better chance of actually being used off-road!

For my part, I was happy to stay 'on road' or at least 'on pavement', as I stepped, still a little gingerly, along even, dry land. My heading was broadly north and I didn't mind being where there were houses and roads. If my experiment that morning were to fail, I thought, then I had a better chance of finding somewhere to recuperate, but I surprised myself when first I checked the time and saw that I had been walking for three hours. Normally, I would have expected to have covered about ten miles in that time, but assessing progress on the map, it seemed more like five. In the next bus shelter (no graffiti) I sat down hoping that neither bus nor people came along, for I did something jolly antisocial, that is to remove shoes and socks and have, like King Cole's musicians, a fine fiddle. My feet were pale and clammy, but not blue. Pressing them was painful but when they were flicked, I felt a tickle, where previously there had been a dull, sensationless thud. All this I interpreted as positive evidence of recovery so, re-shod, I resumed.

Beginning to think that if I weren't on hands and knees by about teatime I could possibly rejoin the Pennine Way that day, I double-checked the maps. It seemed that the easiest way to do get back onto the trail would be to press on, through Halifax, and to pick it up somewhere in Brontë territory, possibly on Haworth Moor. Meanwhile, I contented myself, along the road, by looking out for place names. Ever since I was a very small boy and sporting enthusiast, I had, for example, known of the existence of Elland Road[30] – but until that day, it didn't click that Elland is a small town between Huddersfield and Halifax.

I apologise now, to the residents of Elland, on behalf of everyone south of Watford, for my ignorance! Similarly, I looked for Brighouse and Rastrick,[31] but I couldn't find a signpost which named them together.

Perhaps, like the local authority responsible for replacing road name signs along Abbey Road NW8, who gave up a hopeless fight against souvenir hunters in the years of Beatlemania, the authorities here had decided not to provide temptation for shady, socket set-carrying, night-time operatives with a love of brass band music. Then again, I reflected, perhaps such devious and criminal thoughts only come to people like me!

I stopped to marvel at the head office of the Halifax Building Society, which is centrally and proudly situated in town. They have actually built an 'X'-shaped building to reflect the corporate image.

---

[30] Elland Road is the home of Leeds United Football Club.
[31] The Brighouse and Rastrick Band is regarded by many as the best and most consistent 'public subscription band' in the world.

CHAPTER 7: HUDDERSFIELD – MALHAM

Presumably the architect took his inspiration from the H block prison cells, but I wondered whether the design in front of me was imaginative and rather fun, or the epitome of a corporate marketing world gone mad. I wasn't sure at that time (nor am I now), but I remembered my dismay when informed by my daughter that "M is for chips" (apparently this is common among pre-school children). In my mind's eye I saw a huge McDonald's building, a colossal *M* and modern-world wonder, stretching across the prairie. If there is an *X* in Halifax, I concluded there is sure to be an *M* in America!

Saturday shoppers were busy going about their business, most of them, seemingly, in the opposite direction. Although I felt the odd man out, an observer rather than a participant, I did not feel uncomfortable. People stepped aside, allowing me to get on with what I was doing, without a second glance and, before long, I was standing out of the town feeling as good as I had done for several days. Afternoon sunshine lit the higher, green ground to the west, which seemed as inviting as Black Hill had seemed foreboding. My stride must have lengthened, too, because by 6.00 pm I had reached the Pennine village of Oxenhope, notable for its airy moorland setting and its historic inn, The Gun and Dog.

Inside, the head chef was chalking the board with the specialities of the day. His writing was immaculate; if it were quicker, he could have been a teacher, I thought. The menu looked sumptuous and though I didn't wait to try anything, I have no doubt that if he exercised as much care with his culinary creations as he did with his boardwork, any gastronaut would be in raptures. I did, however, stay long enough to enjoy some excellent ale and chat to locals and visitors who were doing likewise. I was also invited, by a farmer, to camp on his land for the night. He gave me directions, explaining that the Pennine Way went right through his farm. Its location, only some three miles or so to the west, sounded perfect, so I thanked him and agreed to meet him later.

It is perhaps a measure of how my feet were feeling (or perhaps it was the conviviality, the beer, the inspirational scenery or the fine weather) that I decided first to go into Haworth. My diversion added a few more miles but I wanted to revisit this memorable place. In winter it can be bleak, but, on this particular summer evening, it was full of life. Visitors to Haworth drink in The Old Black Bull, and there are even more tearooms and touristy shops than in Holmfirth, for the reason, I imagine, that Cathy and Heathcliff have greater international appeal than Nora and Compo. At the top of the steep and narrow, cobbled main street is the Georgian parsonage in which the Brontë sisters lived, worked and died.

Fish and chips seemed in order that evening, as did a stop at The Wuthering Heights Inn in the village of Stanbury. There I chatted with a couple of Pennine walkers, a publican on holiday from Preston, and the Scandinavian barmaid.

The evening sky was absolutely clear and, once the sun had gone down, I walked the last mile to the farm with my fleece tightly zipped. The farm has an apt name, 'Upper Heights', for it enjoys a commanding and lofty position with terrific views in all directions. Drastically misshapen trees were telltale signs that it can be more than a little bit breezy there, so I took the precaution of pitching my tent in the very corner of the garden, sheltered from the wind by some newly planted conifers. Sure enough, I was woken, in the small hours, by the tops of the young trees thrashing against the roof of the tent.

I unzipped and peeped out. The sky was still clear – it was just extremely windy, but what caught and held my attention was the jet-black sky, free from urban light pollution, and the crystal clarity of the constellations. In order to get an uninterrupted view, I wormed further out of the tent, still in the sleeping bag and lay on my back, on the grass, with only my much-abused feet actually inside. In this unorthodox fashion, I studied the stars, in awe, for at least an hour.

CHAPTER 7: HUDDERSFIELD – MALHAM

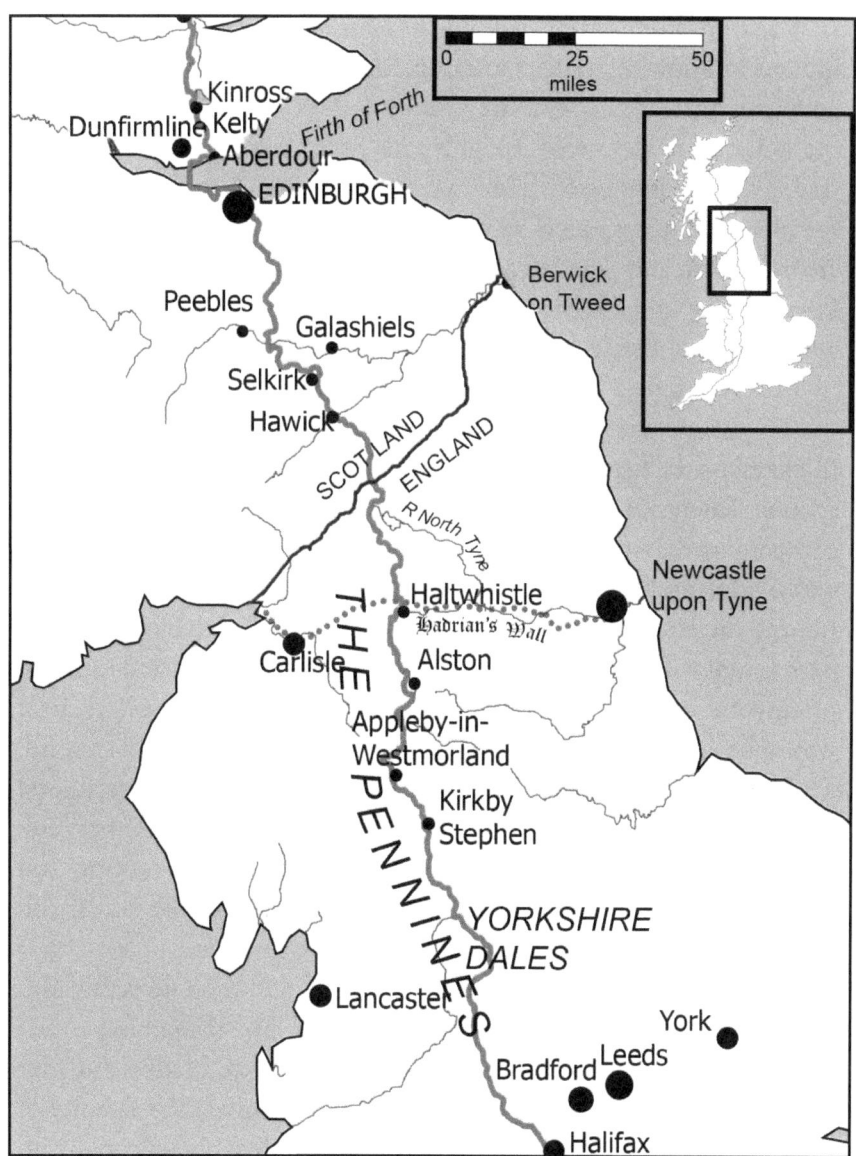

I'll Take the High Road.

There are dozens of farms along the Pennine Way which supplement income by allowing walkers to camp, but my farmer would not accept payment. Instead, he gave me a second clear set of directions to see me well on my way across Keighley Moor. In fact, that section of the trail is clearly signposted. The fingerboards which bear the acorn sign for long-distance paths (I recognised these from the Cotswold Way) are in English and Japanese, and they make plain the directions of the Pennine Way and the Brontë Trail, and how to get to the Brontë Falls, with or without state-of-the-art photographic equipment.

I had chosen to give my big boots another try, since the ground was boggy in places. It was a good choice as, even at half their original thickness, they kept my feet dry and afforded support over broken ground. Safely out of range of the majority of tourists, in lieu of human company there were rabbits, bunting, pipits and plovers aplenty and we all came under the watchful eye of the odd hovering hawk. In fact, I didn't catch sight of any other person *at all* on Keighley Moor. The path is well maintained and the direction clear. It occurred to me that, for anyone wanting to experience a flavour of the Pennine Way, here would be an excellent place to start, certainly better than Black Hill! The terrain is not severe, the views are expansive and there is a good pub, The Black Bull, at Cowling, where you can relax and either look up flowers like Lilliputian lilies (which grow in carpets on limy soil there), or discuss the glacial geology with knowledgeable locals who are proud to live in the Dales.

The path continues over rolling farmland and then descends into the charming village of Lothersdale, where I had something to eat at The Hare and Hounds. As I arrived, radios were blaring out over the car park and inside. It seemed incongruous, given the serenity of the area, until I realised that the landlord was 'live on air', giving an interview about the village and his pub. It sounded idyllic and more or less lived up to his depiction. His wife was not impressed by the excitement, choosing instead to polish the pumps (which she did in a

CHAPTER 7: HUDDERSFIELD – MALHAM

busy fashion quite different in style from that girl in Keynsham) and to talk to me on a range of subjects, including early flowering sweet peas, beer and the River Aire. She also wanted to know why walkers always bought so many Mars bars.

From there I climbed Pinhaw Beacon to take in views of the limestone scenery to the north. On the descent, I remembered that I had forgotten something at the pub. It was a perfectly formed makeshift walking stick which I had picked up in a wood in Brontë country and had been using to ease the load on my sore feet. It may still be there, in the corner of the car park but, if it was taken on by some other Pennine walker, in the painful first week of their challenge, I hope it provided them with some level of relief. Much further on, I met a couple of lads both using a pair of proper walking poles. They explained that in spite of feeling silly to start with, and even though 'your shoulders kill you' after the first day, they thought that the poles were a great help, quoting the manufacturer's claim that up to 30% of the weight and strain is taken off your knees and ankles.

So, unaided, I bounded painfully down into the small village of Thornton in Craven and a couple of miles further on joined the towpath of the Leeds and Liverpool Canal. Having already some experience of canalside walking (shall we say about 200 miles in the previous fortnight) I knew that it was restful and, by and large, flat. Coming down rather than going up was what was hurting me at that point and by following the towpath, albeit much lengthier than the Pennine Way's undulating route, I knew I could reach my objective for that evening relatively painlessly. And so it was that, through long shadows, I came into the busy town of Gargrave.

A further incentive for reaching Gargrave was the prospect of meeting up with an old friend who lives there. She loves cooking much more than hillwalking (we once had a disastrous day in Snowdonia, when Rosalind's vertigo got the better of us), and in order to have supper cooked for me, all I had to do was phone when I reached The

Mason Arms. I confess to feeling frustrated when all I got was a pre-recorded message on the answerphone. I decided to try again later, but what could I do in the meantime? Well, you receive no prizes for guessing that I took the weight off my feet and settled into a pint. I looked around, for it is a really good pub with plenty of character in a fine setting. Perhaps, if this were Rosalind's local, she might be in here, too, I speculated. She wasn't, but lots of other people were, the majority either eating or ordering from an extensive menu. Not wishing to take up a table where four diners might otherwise sit, I moved to the bar and found a stool. A man came in and sat alongside. I nodded.

"Did I need that?" he gasped rhetorically, as he sank the top half of his pint in a single draft.

"You look thirsty," was my somewhat lame reply, but he seemed ready to say something else, and he did:

"I've just driven up from Cornwall!"

His words hit me hard and I had to explain the mixture of irony and depression I felt as his statement snapped me back into the real world.

Of course, if I had thought about it, I would have known that it is perfectly possible to drive from St Ives (as he had just done) to the Yorkshire Dales in a day. It is about 400 miles on trunk roads, so his drive would have been a long one, especially towing his caravan, and he certainly had earned his drink. Nonetheless, I still found it galling to think that in less than a day he had covered what had taken me 23, but he was effusive in his congratulations of my endeavour. The landlord said we had both done well and so that was that. The caravanner imbibed the bottom half and was off, leaving me to talk to the publican.

I was reminded of a devoted parishioner called Paddy who occasionally made reference to his nine sisters, every one of whom had become a nun. This was because I learned that the publican giving

CHAPTER 7: HUDDERSFIELD – MALHAM

the radio interview, back in Lothersdale, was the Gargrave publican's brother. I asked the landlord of The Mason's Arms if he had any other brothers with pubs, but I can't remember his reply, other than that it was curt. I tried the phone again and left another message. I suppose it must have been about eight o'clock and with a rumbling stomach, surrounded by diners, I yielded, not for the first time, you may recall, to the considerable temptation of ordering a large meal.

Somebody told me that there was a campsite nearby, so after one final unsuccessful call, I headed off that way to pitch tent. Having done so, I showered, dumped the rucksack and walked back into town, partly on the off chance of seeing Ros, perhaps in another pub, and partly to see what I could of the attractive market town in the failing light.

The main street is considerably wider than the youthful River Aire, which I had crossed earlier and the buildings are proportionately scaled. I nipped into another pub, The Old Swan, for a nightcap, where a group of cricketers were arguing (I presumed in defeat) as to whether it is better to go 'back and across' or to stand one's ground, when facing fast bowling. I don't suppose they noticed my own cricket shoes (which don't go back and across) nor did I imagine that they would have especially wanted to hear my thoughts, so I kept them to myself. I couldn't help wondering how the easy-going players I had met in Somerset would have fared against these very much more intense Yorkshiremen, were they to meet on the field of play. Could their differences in outlook be reconciled by their shared love of the game? Who could say?

I cannot say whether the stars were bright that night, for I slept soundly, but in the morning the sun was up by the time I awoke at twenty-five past six. Chomping on a packet of biscuits and glugging some cold water, I imagined the cooked breakfast I was surely missing. I could almost smell the bacon sizzling, probably along with black pudding (for regional character) and all the other trimmings. But then I could smell it, distinctly. I looked out and, realising that the cooking smells were coming from the people in the tent 'next door' to mine, decided to cut short the torture by accelerating my packing and heading off back down the canal, before I salivated all over the groundsheet.

The Pennine Way crosses the Leeds and Liverpool Canal by a little bridge at the northern edge of town. Even at that time there were fishermen, dog walkers, joggers and cyclists on the towpath but, before long, I had left them all behind, save for one middle-aged lady who, very spryly, was walking her mutt in the opposite direction. She stopped quietly to watch me clamber awkwardly over a stile and then announced as a matter of fact:

"I take the easy way."

She approached the stile and then easily unlatched a well-oiled but very inconspicuous gate, which swung open with no more than the faintest of shoves and then closed again, under its own weight, just after she and the animal had stepped through.

I came to several more similar fence crossings – now I could spot the gates (it is simple if you use your eyes) – and took the easy way.

At one fence, a yellow and black sign warned of 'Bull in Field'. It was no word of a lie. I saw him before he saw me, so I had half a field's start on him. As I drew nearer, he looked up and snarled, puffing through his nostrils. I stepped purposefully off the path (which ran diagonally across his field) so as to put distance between us. The bull followed me at a bad-tempered walk. Reaching the fence, I scuttled through long grass in the direction of the far stile. I reckoned that if he made a charge, I could throw myself over or through the divide, a prickle or two being preferable to a horn up the rucksack. In the event, the bull must have decided that I wasn't worth the effort, and I got away... only to find his younger brother in the next field but one! He was a veritable enfant terrible and, though a little smaller, craned his neck and roared throatily. He stamped and gestured; I skirted

CHAPTER 7: HUDDERSFIELD – MALHAM

and scuttled … and wondered if it was a bit naughty of the farmer to graze the animals on such a well-trodden pathway. Then again, when I looked on a map from relative safety on the other side of the fence, there were other ways around, such as the track through the nearest village, which is called Bell Busk. It sounded to me a bit like an anagram of 'escape bull', which was a pressing priority and exactly what I had to do!

A work party of people, whom I took to be anglers, were shifting stones in the river. Just there, the Aire is shallow enough that wellies, rather than waders, were the order of the day and it appeared that deeper pools were being created. My guess was that the intention was to make the final hours more comfortable for doomed trout.

Both path and river take convoluted courses. Pennine Way walkers cross from bank to bank a number of times, and there is a gentle climb for a few miles before Malham is reached. This village attracts all manner of visitors and the Buck Inn, the Malham Café, the youth hostel and the Yorkshire Dales National Park Visitor Centre all do great business. I had no need for a bed and so didn't patronise the youth hostel, but on my way from the café to the pub, or from the pub to the visitor centre (I forget which) I passed a lady who was all kitted out for a ramble. From the limping and the agonised expression, I guessed that she must have been feeling like I did way back somewhere around Truro.

"Good morning," I ventured, feeling reasonably sure that it still was. She didn't change her expression and, an instant after passing me, muttered, "Is it?"

For a moment, I felt like going back after the woman and telling her that it would get better and that she shouldn't worry because I felt fine … but I decided that it would sound smug and that she probably wouldn't believe me anyway and that I would very likely end up with a punch on the nose. Accordingly, I took the low moral ground and avoided the issue.

Her obvious anguish gave me cause to reflect on how I had kept myself going in those first painful days by setting myself small goals – the next town, the next pub or even the next lamp-post – and also by keeping in mind the received wisdom that if I could remain ambulatory into the third week, I would probably last the course. Yet here I was, well into that third week, still with sore feet, but feeling strong and tremendously energised, on the brink of the most exciting section of my journey so far.

CHAPTER 8

Malham – Kirkby Stephen

IN WHICH
… I climb many more than thirty-nine steps, learn a lesson in geography, avoid royalty (and the bog), but make a string of horrible mistakes.

I was still exploring the village and had gone up a lane from near the café, when a gent in his garden asked me if I realised that the Pennine Way headed off in a different direction, and he pointed to the north. In hindsight, I'm almost certain that he was trying to be helpful, but especially in the local accent … "D'you know that Pennine Way is down there?" He sounded brassed off and his voice reminded me of an old bat in a pub I once went in, having been gardening, who asked me, in cuttingly sardonic tone, if I realised that they didn't have a public bar! Here, in the Yorkshire Dales, I was pretty sure that I wasn't trespassing, so I thanked him and, a little belligerently, carried on up the lane. I could see lots of walkers down below on the path and not wanting to turn around and walk back past the resident, was glad to see a National Trust footpath signposted to Malham Cove.

My path – for I was alone – contoured the hill to the east and ran broadly parallel and above the main path. I surveyed the two-way parade from a good vantage point. As well as hikers, there were bikers, kids in buggies and lots of dogs, all shuttling between village and the cove. The paths converged at the cove and there I stopped to photograph the spectacle.

Malham Cove is a vast lump of limestone. Perpendicular cliffs, eighty metres high, jut out of the ground, absolutely sheer, in a wide crescent, which overlooks Malham and the green pastures of

Airedale. It is a great draw to rock climbers and abseilers, although there appeared to be many more of the latter than the former. I imagined that, like Gerard Hoffnung's famous funny story about the unfortunate bricklayer who uses a pulley to lower a barrel of bricks which is heavier than he is, heavy human spiders abseiling out of the sky would represent quite a hazard if you were clinging for dear life to a centimetre-wide slither of rock halfway up. Perhaps they have a one-way system. I watched them for a few minutes, stretching my shoulders and back as I did so. I had propped up my pack against a tree. A man came up to me, short and stout, gesturing at the fluorescent sign on the rucksack. He asked in a high-pitched voice:

"Have you *really* come from Land's End?"

I quite liked that sort of question, although it made me think that, if I hadn't really have come from Land's End, it would have been terribly fraudulent to wear that sign ... There again, not everyone who wears a Chelsea shirt plays for Chelsea... so I confirmed that I had. He told me that he had been at Land's End the previous week. I was interested. Had he looked in the End to Enders' register, I enquired. He had, and I told him what I had written. His face lit up.

"So you're the one!"

He said he thought what I had written was funny. I liked this fellow. His questioning continued in the same vein.

"Are you *really* going to John o' Groats?"

It wasn't that he was slow to catch on and although Edmund Blackadder,[32] that notoriously intolerant and sarcastic character, might have answered differently, I tried not to sound long-suffering and said simply:

"That's the idea!"

We stood there watching the brightly coloured sensation-seekers

---

[32] Actor Rowan Atkinson played the lead in the hugely popular TV comedy series *Blackadder*.

kicking off from the rocks as they made their looping descents. If they swapped their garish Lycra for all black and cam cream, it occurred that they could have passed for commandos or extras in a Bond film ... maybe they were!

"What happens if they run out of rope?" It was my turn to ask a silly question. I didn't really expect a reply, nor I think, did I get one, but the man helped me on with my rucksack, asking if he could shake my hand.

It was hardly celebrity status but I climbed the reconstructed path up the side of the cove with a spring in the step, overtaking at least a dozen people who were climbing more slowly, or who had stopped to draw breath at various places. Included in their number were a couple of children counting steps:

"A hundred and fifty-six, a hundred and fifty-seven."

I reckoned that we were less than halfway up, and I made a mental note to ask them how many there were in all, if I saw them at the top. In the event, I was so distracted that, even though I did see them again, I forgot to ask!

Apart from the view, which is awesome, there is an amazing limestone pavement of huge, flat rock, shaped like a cross-section of the cerebellum – but on a gargantuan scale. I jumped from one piece to the next, across deep fissures, which are caused, in time, by the action of mildly acidic rainwater. Sitting on the very edge, with dangling feet, I could see straight down to where the water bubbles out at the source of the river. I let my gaze drift downstream. Malham itself was plain to see but, further back, there was no trace of Gargrave, let alone Thornton, Lothersdale or Cowling, all hidden from view by the hills.

Some of the rocks on top of Malham Cove have been defaced by abseilers in coloured spray paint. There are arrows and numbers which looked as out of place as do the banana skins and orange peel which you always see on popular summits.

North of the cove, there is another geographical textbook example of limestone country, a dry valley. There were cyclists here, too, although it is quite impossible to ride over such broken terrain. These lads carried their bikes on their shoulders (which seemed to me to be defeating the object) but they appeared to be enjoying themselves all the same.

On flatter, more open ground at the top of the dry valley there is a little road, with car parks on either side. I was surprised to see quite so many cars. I spotted an ice cream van, which I approached, thirstily. Neither I nor the ice cream man had any change. I nearly bought five pounds' worth of Mars bars to get around the problem, but didn't. The trader missed out on the sale and I went ahead, even thirstier.

Signposts direct those who come to 'Park and Ramble' in the direction of Malham Tarn, where it is possible to relax by the waterside and study all manner of breeding ducks and geese. I didn't stop, because I knew that ahead of me was a long and strenuous trail across desolate country, and that I would have to maintain momentum in order to reach Horton-in-Ribblesdale before nightfall.

There are places on the high Pennines where you really can survey the whole panorama and not see a single building or living soul, in spite of the fact that an estimated twelve thousand long-distance walkers tread the way each year – as well as many more day walkers. The top of Fountains Fell was one such place. I stopped and stared at the landform ahead of me. Variously described as a crouching lion, a giant bathtub and an upturned boat, the 'mountain' known as Pen-y-Ghent was clear as day, although still some miles in the distance. It looked possible to head directly across springy heather to Pen-y-Ghent, but the path seemed a better bet, even though a look at the map revealed that it snakes wildly. I made good time on the descent from Fountains Fell and reached what I took to be the crouching lion's front paw in about an hour.

Billowing cloud passed high overhead. Feeling a little chill, I reached once more for my fleecy jacket and then began the short climb onto his back. I bounced over duckboards on the boggy approach, laid to prevent erosion along the path. At the summit, I stopped to eat some nutritious dried bananas. A middle-aged couple were already there, enjoying the view and soup, from a thermos. They told me about how people run up Pen-y-Ghent as part of a race known as the 'Three Peaks Challenge'. I said that running up mountains sounded like hard work to me, especially with a heavy load, and we agreed that 'it takes all sorts'. Recreation for one man may seem like torture to another – and I had gathered ample evidence of that.

From the top of Pen-y-Ghent, on the lengthy descent into Ribblesdale, the path is wide and clear. On either side, there is heather but, underfoot, it is stony and relatively unforgiving, if you have sore feet. Not for the first time, however, I passed those whose suffering was greater than my own. In a strange way, this gave me strength and I hustled along, stopping only once to peer down into a pothole. Ghoulishly looking for sheep skeletons, I imagined that, for anyone unfortunate enough to stumble a few paces off the track, perhaps after dark or in fog, it could be a fatal mistake.

By the time I reached the village of Horton, the sun had lost height. Although I felt good for a few more miles, there are no other amenities in the region, so I made straight for the campsite and had set up in time to catch the Pen-y-Ghent Café, before it closed. The proprietor told me more about the Three Peaks Challenge (the other peaks are Ingleborough to the west and Great Whernside to the east). On the café walls, he showed me the winners' Roll of Honour with names and times. It's a course of some twenty-four miles – about the same as my daily average – but what would take me ten or twelve hours all told, takes the champion challengers little more than two!

On the lookout for super-fit fell runners in training, I wandered to the bottom of the village. Finding none, I decided to check out The Crown Hotel, where the overstretched landlady was juggling food orders, beer glasses and room bookings. Horton-in-Ribblesdale is clearly a popular base from which to explore the Dales.

Later on, in the bar of The Golden Lion Hotel, I did some more eavesdropping, on a quiz.

"How long is the Pennine Way?" This time, the publican's voice was unamplified, but his question caught my attention all the same. On this subject, I was well read and I knew that its full length is around 256 miles. Having joined it a little to the north of its start at Edale (and having been forced to divert through Huddersfield) I had calculated that my passage along the Way would be a mere 230 miles. As the crow flies the 'termini' in Derbyshire and the Scottish borders are only 160 miles apart, which says something about the less than direct route the path takes! In the information centre in Horton, I had earlier examined the feasibility of a shortcut, via sections of two other long-distance trails, the Ribble Way and the Dales Way. That night, in my tent, I plotted a new route, cutting more or less due north. My laboured passage through Cornwall had taken me at least a day longer than I had originally scheduled and I sensed that here, in Yorkshire, I had the opportunity to make up that lost time, without compromising on any less of a scenic route. My new plans had got as far as Kirkby Stephen when my torch batteries ran out. This was a good thing, for I was dog-tired and certainly needed my sleep.

I woke at sunrise, a spectacular affair over the roof of the Pennine massif and began what turned out to be probably the most badly mismanaged day of all. My first mistake was being packed and ready to leave Horton (it is pronounced 'Or-n', by the way) a good two hours before the shop was due to open. I had virtually no food – perhaps a solitary dried banana, but decided that I wouldn't wait. After all, I was sure to pass another shop somewhere else, before long ... or so I thought. Foolishly, I ignored the fact that I would be walking through an area which is among the most desolate and sparsely populated in the country.

CHAPTER 8: MALHAM – KIRKBY STEPHEN

Over the first few miles, following the River Ribble, I saw no one at all. I did see an occasional farm building, usually in the distance, as well as plenty of sheep and rabbits, but there were definitely no shops, so I had to sustain myself with magnificent views back to Pen-y-Ghent and across over Ingleborough Hill. I crossed the road to Hawes (not taking it was my next mistake) and climbed onto Blea Moor which, for squelchiness, runs Black Hill a close second. By this time I had picked up waymarkers on the Dales Way and the path was well-trodden, right up to the place where a large sign stopped me in my tracks, warning:

'DANGER! DEEP BOG'

It was clear that straight ahead was not the way to go, although to my alarm, there were footsteps going into the middle of the bog and not, as far as I could discern, coming out again! Had some hapless Dale walker come to a premature watery grave on his way to the Lakes? It certainly seemed so. I was momentarily distracted by loud shouts from across the valley where a couple of farmhands on quad bikes were herding sheep. Weighed down by my heavy rucksack, I started to sink, completely lost my cool and thrashing and splashing, stumbled backwards, eventually coming to some firmer ground. I sat down on a stone and re-examined the problem, scraping black ooze from my legs with finger and thumb. A wide diversion was required and I chose the higher ground to the left of the bog, wishing I had done so in the first place.

Others must have survived the perils of the bog, because bootprints rejoined the track a little further on, where it descends to a minor road, on which I was most surprised to meet a police motorcade with outriders and cars escorting a Range Rover with darkened windows. Bedraggled and black from the bog, I was in no state to receive royalty, so I waved them through.

The road wriggles down and down, through impressive arches of one of several viaducts which carry the Pennine railway dramatically on its way to Carlisle. My stomach was rumbling badly as I came to a tiny settlement served by a pub, The Sportsman, which advertised 'Good Food'. "Good! Food," I thought but, when I tried the door, found it locked. Having cross-checked the opening times, a glance at my scratched watch confirmed the worst. Making my next mistake, I decided not to wait the half-hour or so for the doors to open. My map showed that there was another settlement about a mile further on, doubtless offering something for the hungry walker. Reaching Cowgill, I found about two houses and a telephone box (my wife remembered me calling and announcing, "I'm in the middle of nowhere!"). As neither of the houses were public ones, I continued, rather than double back, up onto the fells again.

On the very steep lane out of Cowgill, I met some other walkers, including a couple of slightly built girls, loaded down with packs almost as large as my own. They walked at a terrific pace, which was too hot for me. I couldn't keep up, but they were keen to tell me about a wonderful place to stay in the village of Dent, further down the valley. As the gap between us widened, our conversation continued in shouts, but I never did quite catch the name of the place. I wanted to tell them that they couldn't expect to keep marching at the speed of Gurkhas, but they were gone. Moments later, I realised the reason for their haste, when I spotted a very unlikely railway station, from where, if they caught the train, they could return home, I presumed. It all seemed a long way removed from the working morning scuttle up Station Approach in Commuterland.

I came across another danger sign near there, only this time I knew that it could be ignored in safety:

U5509 Lea Yeat to Garsdale. Altitude 1750ft.

Winter conditions can be dangerous.

Under a scorching sun, I toiled higher and I could quite see how it would be the toboggan ride of a lifetime in snow. At the highest point

CHAPTER 8: MALHAM – KIRKBY STEPHEN

on the crossing, I could clearly make out the mountains of Cumbria (the Langdale Pikes lie about thirty miles to the west) and I rested for a while. Thinking it would be a perfect place for a picnic, if I had one, I reached for the water bottle and made short work of the few fluid ounces within. A warm breeze pushed across me from the west. It was like facing a hairdryer on low power – not altogether unpleasant and quite a change, I thought, from conditions on Black Hill only a few days before.

I was high above the railway, which had disappeared into a long tunnel, but I saw from the map that my path and the track were due to converge at Garsdale Head, where there was a station – perhaps with a drinks or chocolate machine. It had neither, nor had the settlement any shop or pub. It appeared to consist of nothing but small, grey houses which I took to have been originally intended for railway workers.

Dehydrated by the heat and breeze, my hunger by this stage was overtaken by a powerful thirst. My tongue felt swollen and dry and I had resolved to knock on the door of the next house I came to when I spotted a pub in the distance on the main road which links Kendal to Hawes. It was not a mirage: I could plainly see drinkers enjoying their refreshment on the patio courtyard to the side. Some cool cider would quench my thirst, I thought ... and no doubt I would be able to get something to eat. Then I checked the time. It was three minutes to two. Alarmed at the possibility they might stop serving food at two o'clock, I hitched up the pack as high as it would go and broke into a run. As do marathon runners, with the finishing line in sight, I picked up my step and reached the entrance at a few seconds to two.

The landlord was turning off lights. My heart sank ... but perhaps he could be persuaded:

"Would you mind terribly if ..." I began grovellingly.

"I'm sorry, we're closed."

"But please ..."

"No, I'm sorry, I've got to go," and he did, ushering me out at the same time.

Now I do confess at first to feeling aggrieved, especially since the locals outside had full pints, but any resentment I had was soon put aside, when I learned that the reason for the abrupt closure was motivated not by a dislike of backpacking Southerners, but because his daughter had been taken seriously ill and he was rushing to her side.

At the road junction there, a sign showed that Hawes, with all its cafés and shops, was just four and a half miles to the south-east. I could already have been there, I mused, had I taken the other road ... or, for that matter, if I'd stayed on the Pennine Way. Another sign confirmed that the next place, Kirkby Stephen was 11 miles to the north. Going west, there was no settlement at all for even further and, with no footpaths or tracks around, I was faced with a bleak choice: Hawes or Kirkby Stephen. Neither route particularly appealed but my eventual decision was made on the grounds that by heading north, I would at least be heading in the direction of John o' Groats and not Dover.

A telephone engineer was digging, energetically, at the rocky ground by the roadside a little way up the road. Leaning on his spade to draw breath, he asked me where I was heading. Strangely, he said, he had spoken to someone else, a couple of weeks back, doing the same thing that I was. Wondering whether the other 'end to ender' reached his destination and wondering, more acutely, whether I would reach Kirkby Stephen without expiring, I hesitatingly enquired as to whether I could expect to come across any place of refreshment along that road.

His reply prompted me to sigh and say something like, "Ah well ..." In my head, my unvoiced thoughts were less reserved, for I knew that I was in trouble.

Eleven straight miles ought to have taken me in the region of three

CHAPTER 8: MALHAM – KIRKBY STEPHEN

hours, on a good day. This was not a good day and, in the event, it took nearly five hours. I had already carried my pack for twenty-two miles, over strenuous ground, on an empty stomach. I was incredibly thirsty and boiling hot. What's more, the telephone man was right and the settlements of Aisgill and Outhgill, below the evocatively named Wild Boar Fell, are little more than the odd farm building. On the door of one house was even a notice which read:

"Sorry, No Tea – not even for cyclists".

In fact, I met one such thirsty cyclist. He stopped to ask if he could buy some chocolate. Walkers always carry chocolate, he had convinced himself, and he took some persuading that this particular walker had none. By this stage, I was down to a snail's pace and it was a good thing I was, otherwise I might have missed my redemption, which came in the form of a hedgerow supporting wild raspberries, deliciously sweet and flavoursome. Exactly as I had done, when desperate, in Cornwall, I fell upon this godsend like a child on an illicit biscuit raid, gratefully gorging what must have been hundreds.

Somewhat revitalised and probably with stained and sticky chin (I had not thought to carry a vanity mirror) I emerged from the bushes to walk the next few miles without seeing a soul.

The River Eden flows along that valley, although it is not immediately accessible until a couple of miles south of Kirkby Stephen, where a wide meander skirts a grassy area by the road, popular with picnickers. I knelt by the bank and plunged my head right into the cool, clear water for an instant, which was enough. I gasped and blew, then shook like a wet dog, spraying droplets to either side and then repeated the therapy. Next it was the feet, which were released from their encapsulation and immersed until they ached from cold. I flopped back onto my overturned rucksack and closed my eyes, my feet now positioned so that only my toes received a gentle splashing from the fast-moving water every now and again. I drifted into a sleep, induced by exhaustion and ecstatic sensory overload.

Between there and the outskirts of Kirkby Stephen, I had the good fortune to come across a little filling station which was not only open, but well stocked with chocolate and drinks. I also came across a pub, The Black Bull, to which I returned later in the evening, as well as a fully equipped campsite.

Most of any campsite is taken up with 'caravanners' but, of the 'tenters', at this one, the majority seemed to be walking, or cycling the coast-to-coast route which runs from Robin Hood's Bay to St Bees and crosses the country at that point. As I sat in the laundry room, a young man asked me directly:

"Are you on Wainwright's Coast to Coast?"

"No," I replied and then, thinking that this might seem abrupt, I added, "…but I am walking coast to coast, in a sense."

"How do you mean?" He sat up straighter, in the plastic chair, and I explained. He listened and then asked:

"How long has it taken you to get this far?"

"About three weeks."

"That's good going! It's taken us a fortnight to get from Robin Hood's Bay."

He was in a group of six (three of each gender) and was surprised to hear that I was going solo.

"Don't you get lonely, walking on your own?"

I hesitated and thought.

"No. There's always something to see or think about – and you can go at your own pace."

"How about the distance, doesn't that bother you?" This was turning out to be quite a penetrating interviewer. I thought some more.

"No, not really, it's more the passage of time." Thinking about that road sign saying 'Kirkby Stephen 11', I tried to explain what I meant, adding: "If you walk at three miles an hour, for ten hours, you've walked thirty miles …"

CHAPTER 8: MALHAM – KIRKBY STEPHEN

"But you've walked all day!" He was right and at the risk of labouring the point, I was about to say what happens when you walk all week and so on, when the tumble dryer came to an end.

As he reached inside, feeling his washing, I nobly stressed that if it wasn't perfectly dry, he should put in another 50p and that I didn't mind waiting longer.

"It's all yours!" he announced and, cramming socks into a bag, he disappeared back to his friends.

Having loaded my own stuff into the machine, I, too, returned to my tent, which happened to be within easy earshot of the lad's. To my great amusement, I heard him begin to regale his chums about our meeting. I zipped up my tent; there is little privacy when tenting in a fairly crowded area, and listened.

"I've just met this bloke," he began, "who is walking from Land's End to John o' Groats. It's only taken him three weeks so far and he says it's not the distance but the passage of time. Come to think of it, he did look rather odd!"

"What do you mean?" asked a friend.

"Well ..." (I waited) "... he did ask if I wanted to use the tumble dryer again before him." Their conversation moved on and I thought to myself that I had probably got off quite lightly if that was the oddest thing about me he could think of saying!

It is an extraordinary fact, and quite beyond my explanation, that I went for a run that evening. I can only think that my body needed to break free from the walking rhythm and that without big boots and heavy pack I could stretch out to a greater extent. Enjoying the sunset, I tested my newly toned leg muscles and it felt good.

CHAPTER 9

Kirkby Stephen – Hadrian's Wall

IN WHICH
...in the footsteps of Roman legionnaires, I search for a maiden but find a poet, and fall in the Tyne.

Not wishing ever again to go foodless all day (at least when putting the body under such strain) I stocked up, on my way out of Kirkby Stephen, in the morning. Having done so, my pack was rather too heavy, but the walking was gentle, through lanes and paths in the Eden Valley. Mid-morning, I stopped, and was leaning at the foot of a fingerboard road sign, eating cheese, when a car pulled up and I was asked directions to the village of Soulby.

Not only had I just walked through Soulby, but the road sign clearly showed the way, so, instead of pointing them along the road, I pointed above my head to the sign. I didn't have to say anything but ruminated as I continued masticating, whether it was unkind to highlight their lack of observation ... but concluded only that it is probably true that we are all very unobservant. Living those last weeks, on my wits, in the country (and my daily success or failure being so heavily dependent on being able to find my way), was teaching me to open my eyes. If I could spot partially concealed church spires on the horizon, detect the rumble of a distant railway, or notice the diffused light from street lamps of hidden settlements in the next valley, then I would rarely miss as big a directional clue as a signpost – at least it seemed like that to me at the time.

I approached the busy market town of Appleby in Westmorland via one particular footpath, past allotments where nettles whose height and intensity threatened for a while to challenge those on the

CHAPTER 9: KIRKBY STEPHEN – HADRIAN'S WALL

Severn Way, but where the path became better trod, they were fewer, and I reached the town in relative comfort.

The pubs and cafés were doing good business. I sought refreshment at an establishment in Boroughgate called A'board Inn. Sitting outside beneath colourful hanging baskets of fuchsias and trailing lobelia I just watched people coming and going. What seemed to me to be a healthy local population was undoubtedly swollen by a good number of visitors, although, I imagined, not the droves which flock to relatively nearby places like Windermere. Had I arrived a few weeks earlier, however, I doubt whether I would have got a seat at all. Appleby's famous horse fair, held each year in June, attracts gypsies and visitors from all Britain, as well as from overseas. At the top of the street is the castle, with its splendid Norman keep. Coachloads of tourists gathered outside and a human stream trickled from there down the street, in and out of shops and onwards, in the direction of the Moot Hall, which is 16th-century, and the cloistered St Lawrence's church. Strangely, only a fraction of their number appeared to be making the return journey up Boroughgate back towards the castle.

I contemplated the location of Appleby. The town's claim to be at 'the bullseye of Britain' is at least partly justified. I remembered thinking how the 'Midlands' are assuredly not 'in the middle'. Here, I could draw satisfaction from the knowledge that, from the Scillies, I was now at least halfway to Shetland!

Needing more shade than the hanging baskets could provide, I went inside and engaged the bar staff in conversation. I wanted to find out more about the town and they (the landlord and a student named Emma, whose fresh face and agile mind left quite an impression on me) were happy to chat, in between pulling pints and passing food orders to the kitchen.

I asked about the Roman road, along which I had walked and was not altogether surprised to be informed that the whole region is rich in Roman history. When subjugating the Brigantes was the name

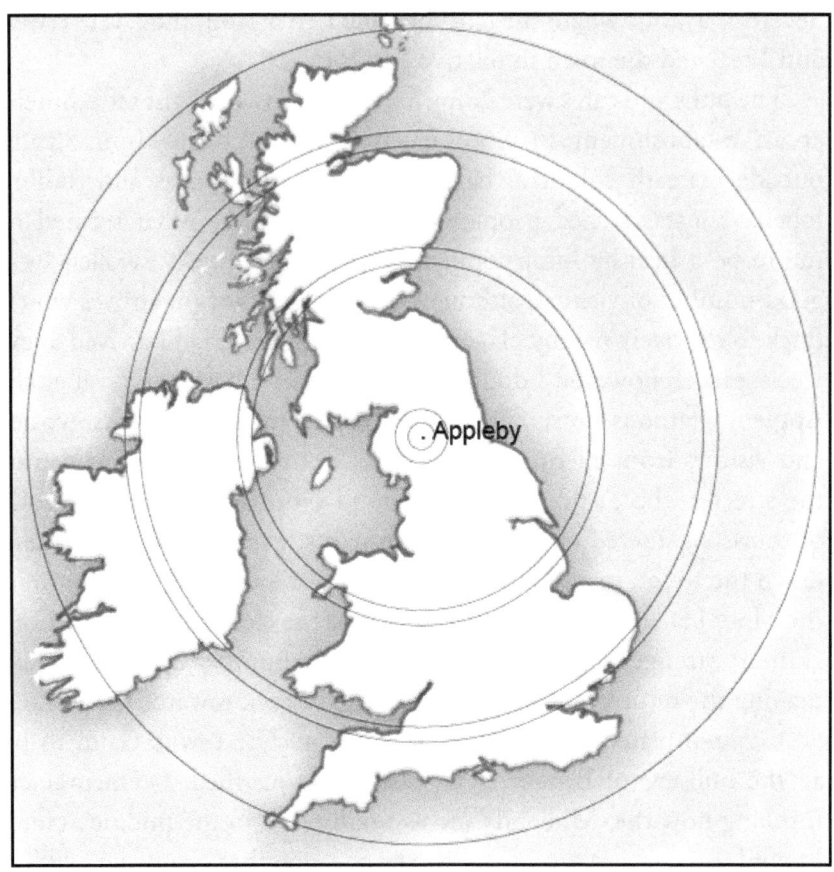

Appleby. At Britain's bullseye?

of the game, troops and supplies travelled along Ermine Street and at nearby Kirkby Thore, branched directly towards Hadrian's Wall. I heard that much of the way is still in evidence... and walkable, so I fixed upon the idea of checking it out.

I could not recall ever having been to Appleby in Westmorland before – perhaps as a child, but it struck me as the sort of place I should revisit. Whether or not it was true, it seemed to be the first place of any size that I had come to without previous memory of

CHAPTER 9: KIRKBY STEPHEN – HADRIAN'S WALL

having been there at some other time in my life. I knew I had never been to John o' Groats, nor anywhere further north than Inverness, but here, too, I got a strong sense of stepping into the unknown – and my level of excitement rose another notch.

My level of sleepiness also rose when, having decided to picnic by the river, I stretched out on the warm grass, loosened my boots and closed my eyes.

I woke around three and, for the rest of the afternoon, strolled north-westwards along the gentle lanes of Eden Vale through a number of farming villages with names like Long Marton, Blencarn and Skirwith, coming at sunset to Ousby, which had the double appeal of having a campsite and a pub. Furthermore, its position at the foot of the fells was perfect for what I had in mind for the following day.

Doubtless having somehow got wind of my imminent arrival, the management of the pub had kindly arranged for a large-scale map of the area to be glazed and mounted on the wall. I studied the paths and fixed on the idea of climbing Melmerby Fell to join the course of Maiden Way somewhere on Alston Moor. The map confirming what I had been told earlier, as it looked feasible to follow the Roman road all the way to Hadrian's Wall about twenty-five miles to the north. That was the plan anyway.

It was a beautifully clear morning and I made good progress up a couple of rising farm tracks. I paused to look back across the fields to the west. In the distance, I could easily see the Cumbrian Mountains and was busy identifying the Langdale Pikes when a very large hare popped out of the grass below me. I stood very still as he paused to assess the danger. He did not strike me as being a particularly intelligent hare, for he made his escape by bolting towards me and uphill, passing almost within bagging distance. What he lacked in sense, he certainly made up for in speed, for he climbed the steep bank above the path at a pace which was astonishing... even fabulous.

On the boggy fell top, I could not, for the life of me, find any

Roman road. This surprised me, because I must have actually crossed its path at some point. There were several tracks, mostly which appeared to have been made by a caterpillar-tracked agricultural vehicle, but no sign of a paved ancient highway. Perhaps it was naïve of me not to realise that the same stones now, more than likely, make walls and support farm buildings in the area. Even so, I was vexed that this maiden had given me the slip. I caught sight of another walker. Perhaps he could help, so I tried to catch up with the fellow. Like the hare, this individual was making very rapid progress across the moor and in the end I gave up the chase near a place I took to be the source of the River Tyne. I drank the clear water where the river was narrow enough to stand with one foot on either side. You couldn't do that at Jarrow, I thought.

With the other walker long gone, I was once more completely alone. Although decidedly breezy, it was warm, for which I was thankful. It needed little imagination to picture an altogether bleaker scene up there, perhaps in fog or hail. My map showed that if I continued trekking eastward, I would eventually return to the Pennine Way as it heads down into the village of Garrigill, where I would surely find local amenities. Alternatively, I could follow the South Tyne down on either side of the water but, as the stream became stronger, there were places where the banks were too steep or too boggy and the protruding stones too few. Several times I had to haul myself up and away from the rushing current, by tugging on couch grass and scrambling on hands and knees, before sliding back to the waterside to continue, painfully slowly, downstream.

Eventually the inevitable happened and, marooned midstream on a rock, I lunged onto an unstable boulder which shot me headlong into the water. As I fell, the weight of the rucksack pulled me sideways, resulting in almost total immersion for walker and kit alike. I recovered to a kneeling position in which I remained for some time, dripping and stunned, with the cold water rushing around my nether

CHAPTER 9: KIRKBY STEPHEN – HADRIAN'S WALL

regions. I recalled the working party of fishermen whom I had seen wading in the Aire. If they could see me now, I thought, it would be their turn to wonder what was going on!

I stumbled right across the river to the opposite bank, which was gentler, being on the outside of a curve, and sat down. I seemed to be unhurt, save for a twisted wrist (not the one which the dog bit) and in any case my thinking at that time was 'better a wrist than an ankle'. Though my clothes were wet, the fabric layering and plastic bag filing system within my rucksack had, to a good degree, kept the South Tyne out. Remarkably, deep in an inner sanctum, I found some bone dry socks and my cricket shoes. My fleece, too, was dry, although it was far too hot a day to wear that, so I opted instead for dry feet and the same shorts and top. It would be a test for those garments, because the manufacturers claim that they dry in minutes – so I did some wringing out and pulled my shirt clammily over my body.

After a few more ups and downs, I caught sight of traffic on the main road linking Penrith and Alston. If I could cut across the moor to it, I reasoned, there was less chance of another soaking. In the event, the ground was extremely boggy, and instead of jumping from boulder to boulder by (or in) the river, I found myself jumping from clump to tufty clump of couch grass, to avoid sinking knee-deep in black ooze. The comic episode on Alston Moor ended when, at the very edge, I was held up for some while trying hurriedly to fix a farm gate which had collapsed when I tried to open it. Once on the road, I made rapid progress into the town. What with the afternoon sun and my exertions, my clothes were almost dry and only the most observant or curious would have noticed the steam still rising from my torso as I marched across the square towards the chip shop.

Alston is the highest market town in England and its character seems to reflect this, because it serves a hardy people. The shops stock welly boots and thermal underwear, but there is also enough width in the main square for a coach party or two to alight. One group I mingled with had driven up from Bradford. They had an hour to 'do' Alston before pressing on to 'do' Hadrian's Wall before supper. I felt relieved not to be tied down to such a pressing schedule and, in spite of wasting so much time on the moor, I knew I could afford to explore a little or to relax, as I did in The Swan's Head.

In the early evening, refreshed and almost dry, I stepped outside rather creakily and paced down again through the town, which was bathed in a silvery yellow light. The streets were rather less busy and I noticed that the coach had gone. I thought of its passengers and the relative proximity of Hadrian's Wall. It represented quite a landmark in my journey. The sightseers would probably already have reached this landmark in air-conditioned comfort, but still I did not envy them. I knew it would take me rather longer, but I felt as if nothing could stop me. From the moor, I had looked over to the Cumbrian Mountains earlier in the day but I had seen something else as well which now filled my thoughts. One line of hills, on the horizon, may look pretty much like another but, to the north, the faint forms I made out were very different – they were Scottish hills. It was beginning to hit me that my march the length of England was nearing an end, and that the start of a new adventure was almost within reach.

It would have been possible for me to stay that night in Alston, but it seemed right to 'chip off' a few more miles, so I followed my old friend the Pennine Way, along the South Tyne, as far as Slaggyford, where I camped on a midgy caravan site right by the river.

The warden tried, unsuccessfully, to save me an additional three miles' round trip to the only hostelry in or near Slaggyford.

"There's no pub 'round 'ere," she growled. "You'd best lay up."

I said that I would allow my rucksack to lay up, or down, or something, at which she looked perplexed ... but gave me directions all the same.

I had in mind meeting some local people who could tell me about farming, more about the Romans, or the history of lead mining in the

CHAPTER 9: KIRKBY STEPHEN – HADRIAN'S WALL

area, but the barman was a Londoner and the only other customers were a young couple on holiday from Kent (who postponed their early night to swap stories with me) and a motorbike enthusiast, also from the Home Counties, who had recently moved north to 'get away from it'! I had an idea what 'it' might have been. Like me, he enjoyed the wind in his hair ... although he had rather more of it than me!

If, in the pub, I had missed out on matters of local culture, then I was more than compensated in the morning, when I attempted to return the shower block key to the warden. In a surprise move, she revealed herself to be not only an expert on the region, but also of profoundly artistic temperament.

"They call me the 'Slaggyford Poet'".

We went on a tour of the site and she pointed out handwritten verses, pinned to trees and dustbins, or dangling from raspberry bushes. Here and there were snapshots, polythene-wrapped against the wet, showing the river in the different seasons. I was interested and easily persuaded her to recite some of her work. Her voice was incredibly low (she could have sung baritone) and she referred to the river as 'her beloved'. At first, her eyes followed the words on the sheet, but then they moved away as she continued. The Slaggyford Poet wept as she spoke; were I not the emotionally stilted product of public school education, I believe I might have wept, too!

With the sound of Mrs Mill's deep voice still resonating inside my head and, for the most part, within earshot of the babbling river, I walked well that morning, making good time in the footsteps of Roman legionnaires along the illusive Maiden Way, which, eventually, had become obvious. I dropped down into Haltwhistle for something to eat and was hugely impressed by the lengths that town had recently gone to in creating an attractive and safe place to walk, or enjoy leisure time, by the river and away from the fast and furious A69.

It was up a much less busy thoroughfare that I left the town, one so steep that it put me in mind of a student route on the hilly campus at Exeter, which we used to call 'Cardiac Hill'. Another credit for the town planners at Haltwhistle, benches, had been positioned at intervals on the ascent, so one could 'take a breather' or enjoy the view. As a hardening and self-respecting "End to Ender", I couldn't really do anything other than shun the opportunity... but I do confess to being tempted. At times like that, the pack did feel heavy!

The long haul was worth it, for at the top was not only a pub, The Milecastle, but also, running straight as an arrow, the East-West Roman service road and beyond it Hadrian's Wall itself, northern frontier of Roman Britain and the edge of an empire. Beyond that, well, Caledonia, wild kingdom of the barbarous Picts! What adventure it promised!

A staggering amount of rock was used, in the region of four million tonnes, in the wall's construction. At one time, it stood considerably higher than it does today (large sections have been reconstructed) but Hadrian's Wall is still an impressive structure. It was easy to see how this linear barrier, which stretched nearly eighty miles from the outskirts of Newcastle to the Solway Firth, must have inspired awe on both sides... and now it inspired my awe.

I crossed the road and climbed up to the structure itself. As I sat against the wall, with the sun on my face, two things struck me. Firstly, what a marvellous suntrap it made (at its full height of perhaps fifteen feet, all the more so), and that here was the sunny Roman Empire ... On the other side, dark, shadowy territory. I also thought of what a stunning piece of bureaucracy the whole project represented – one imperial decision to consolidate, rather than to expand, and nearly two thousand years on, this was the result!

I followed its course eastwards, to the point where it passes The Twice Brewed Inn. Partly because of its location and partly because of a good experience the previous year, this pub represented a mile-marker in my own planning. According to the story, General Wade took a break here from co-ordinating road building across the

CHAPTER 9: KIRKBY STEPHEN – HADRIAN'S WALL

country, to complain that his beer was too weak, instructing that it be brewed again. Presumably, he knew more about engineering than he did about fermentation! Nevertheless, The Twice Brewed Inn was to be my next port of call.

Enjoying a break from the heat and fiercely bright sunlight, I sipped a drink and got chatting to a retired scientist, if there can be such a thing, named Robert Craig. At eighty-eight years of age, he was still touring the country, to seek out new hills to climb and historic sites to visit. In great detail, he told me of his theories about the density of resins within the structure of decaying pine logs in Loch Ness and how his findings had been published in *Scientific American*. His investigations, it seems, constitute the principal body of evidence on which are hinged arguments of many a Nessie[33] sceptic. When I suggested that it could be the monster pushing the logs about, the venerable old boy offered to buy me another drink!

There is a visitor information centre just to the south, where I genned up on Hadrian's Wall and the Northumberland National Park, before returning to the wall and what turned out to be an eventful episode.

---

[33] Nessie, a.k.a. the Loch Ness Monster certainly exists – ask anyone involved in Scottish tourism or merchandising in the area.

CHAPTER 10

Hadrian's Wall – Carter Bar

IN WHICH
…as I near the Scottish Border, one false step causes a helicopter to be scrambled and I rue the downgrading of my first aid kit.

It began quietly enough. I climbed a succession of ramparts, gaining height and losing company in a pattern which was by now familiar, mirrored wherever tourists throng near to areas of wild country or upland, until I was once more alone. The views were terrific and I had stopped to take a photo or two when I caught sight of something which caused me to put the camera away. Ahead, in the distance, a man was lying at the foot of the wall and was waving an arm in signal to me. I guessed at once that he had fallen and needed help.

Laden as I was, it was virtually impossible to run up a one-in-four gradient, over broken ground, but I did my best. He had indeed been scrambling on the wall and had landed awkwardly as he fell. His right arm was clearly broken, above the wrist, and he was in shock.

"I feel so stupid," he said, not once, but about five times, in a shaky and apologetic voice. It was true that the wall at that point was only around two metres high, but the ground where he lay was rocky and uneven. I attempted to reassure the patient by telling him that parachutists normally land with a force equivalent to having jumped from a six-foot wall … and that plenty of parachutists break their ankles or legs, even their backs. He groaned and shuddered and I wondered whether I should continue on that tack.

I knew that he would have to get down from the moor; that much was easy to work out. How this could be done was another matter.

CHAPTER 10: HADRIAN'S WALL – CARTER BAR

He was loath to move at all and not having a great deal of first aid experience (treatment of blisters aside) I was reluctant to start pulling him about. The situation was not desperate, however. For one thing, it was a warm, sunny afternoon – this mountain rescue would not be hampered by blizzards or failing light. In addition, I was reasonably well equipped, because, although back on Dartmoor, good old Henry had stripped my first aid box of the very item I most needed (his words resonated in my head: "triangular bandage, you'll never need that!"). I did have painkillers with me and my lightweight thermal sleeping bag was ideal for putting over the man. A third thing was in our favour – I could see a farmhouse a little way below us. I felt sure that others would pass before long, for it is popular hiking country and we decided that I should go there to call an ambulance. Leaving my pack at his side, I bounded down the hill and in no time had reached the farmhouse.

A lady answered my knock before I had a chance to worry that there might be nobody at home and we dialled 999. Hexham is not far by road and it seemed likely that an ambulance might be despatched from there. I puffed back up to the wall where, sure enough, another person had arrived and was keeping the fellow talking.

"The ambulance is on its way!" I announced with a certain satisfaction. The man nodded and grimaced. "It won't be long."

In truth, I had no idea how long it would be but the words just popped out in the same way that I imagine GPs can't prevent themselves from asking: "What seems to be the problem?" dozens of times a day.

To my surprise, the next thing was the arrival of a rescue helicopter. As it approached, I climbed up onto the wall and waved my arms, as people do in disaster movies. It circled, looking for somewhere to land (I presumed) and then flew off, down the hillside and out of sight, to where I believe it landed. Meanwhile, the vehicle from Hexham had reached the farmhouse and within about five or ten minutes a paramedic approached, accompanied by a family who were helping to carry his equipment, as he was somewhat tubby and badly out of breath. Blowing and blaspheming colourfully, the ambulance man made me think of my judo teacher back in schooldays, certainly not for the tubbiness, not for the blowing out of breath, but because of his language: when I once told my judo teacher that I couldn't attend class one evening because I had to revise for a Latin exam the next day, he informed me that he himself spoke two languages, fluently – "good" and "bad"…and then proved it, demonstrating his displeasure at my lack of commitment to the martial art!

Back at the foot of Hadrian's Wall, the paramedic mopped his perspiring brow, drew breath, stopped swearing and then, with calm authority, began work on the injured man. I jumped down, carefully, from the wall and watched. Certain checks having been made, the arm was moved gently and put in a sling. Several people, at the ambulance man's word, helped the "fall guy" to his feet. He faltered for a moment but then, a step at a time, headed off down the hillside with his good arm bound to the ambulance man, as would a front-row forward in a rugby scrum… And that was that: I never knew his name, nor very much about him, but I was pleased to have been able to help in some way. As I repacked my rucksack, I looked to see if the helicopter would reappear. It didn't, at least in the time that I was there. In fact, I can't be sure whether the fellow continued his journey to hospital by air or on the road; either way, he, too, would have a story to tell.

For my own part, all the excitement had set me back by a couple of hours. I had planned to camp at Bellingham, a good three to four hours' march to the north. I knew that I would have to hurry to reach there before dark, so I didn't linger. Leaving the wall near Housesteads Fort, I followed the acorn signs north across open ground and into Wark Forest, where tree felling sent the Pennine Way on an irritating diversion. Notices of the 'Application for Planning Permission' type were posted at various points. I didn't read all the detail but picked up one point about providing what was referred to as 'a sustainable alternative route'.

CHAPTER 10: HADRIAN'S WALL – CARTER BAR

Hadrian's Wall.

Pen-y-Ghent – crouching lion or upturned boat?

Just there, the way crossed boggy ground, and it was clear that the volume of traffic along that section was taking its toll. I could sympathise but, at that stage, I would have been thankful of a good, direct route to the campsite.

Some miles further along and beyond that particular section of coniferous plantation, I stopped to watch the sun going down. I had the notion that this might be my last English sunset for a while, and it was a good one. As the cells of my retina overdosed on crimson and orange, I reflected on the day's events. For his sake, I hoped that man I had helped had cleared the plaster room by then and was not further detained, awaiting 'pegging' or manipulation. "Ouch," I thought and looked ahead in the direction of Scotland. With wild and lonely miles before me – not to mention some pretty serious mountains, I knew that I would have to be careful. I thought back to my stumble into the Tyne and, feeling my wrist, which was no more than a little tender, I realised how lucky I had been. It could have ended up very differently. "Literally one false step…": it was a sobering thought.

There was still some way to go before I reached Bellingham. I recall pleasant walking across undulating pasture. A couple of the farmsteads were offering camping and had deployed the same tactical psychology I have seen at filling stations which advertise: "Last petrol before motorway". Weary walkers were informed: "Next Youth Hostel 7 miles". I was tempted but, as I could still see where I was going, decided to press on. Eventually, from the top of a craggy hill by a radio mast, the town came into view. Guided by Bellingham's orange street lamps, this particular ship came into port.

The dew on my tent had already burnt off by the time I came to roll it up. Any fool could have told that it was going to be another scorcher – but *this* fool didn't think to take extra water. Fluids are a heavy component of the backpacker's load. I usually carried a litre in my bottle and would top up during the day, if I had chance. Occasionally, I bought fizzy drinks or mineral water and would recycle lightweight

CHAPTER 10: HADRIAN'S WALL – CARTER BAR

empties with secure caps as reserve water carriers... but not that day. Half my water was gone by the time I reached the top of Padon Hill about 6 miles out of Bellingham. I was burning up and sought shade at one time by lying up against a stone wall. The sun was so high that the wall cast only a few centimetres of shadow. I lay there for the best part of an hour and saw no one, until a middle-aged couple came along heading southwards. They, too, had overheated and lay down against the wall. I observed that, to the hovering hawk above us, we must have looked like a string of coloured sausages in the middle of his hunting grounds. There was more shade ahead – and plenty of it, for only a couple of miles from that place, the Pennine Way plunges into the Kielder Forest, which is Britain's largest.

Most of the Forestry Commission tracks are broad and straight as their primary use is, of course, to provide access for the workforce with their giant logging vehicles. There are no views to speak of, because the planting is dense. As if at the bottom of a deep trench, I walked beneath a narrow band of sky, and when a mightily laden truck came grinding by, the whole corridor was filled with dust.

Not only did the swarms of mosquitoes disappear (they breed in the stagnant drainage ditches), but also the murk was so thick that I couldn't see through it clearly enough to count the number of trunks being hauled – it could have been upwards of thirty.

I made reasonable time along these paths, though I cannot say I enjoyed the experience greatly. With my water bottle all but dry, I rationed myself to a sip a mile, which I took after every seventeen minutes' walking. I started to work out how many trees there are in all: the whole of the Border Forest Park covers about 250 square miles ... but I got bored with the calculation at that point. If anyone wants to know, my answer would be: "Lots!"

Eventually, I came out of the trees near Byrness and made for the hotel, which is known as the only place on the last 45 miles of the Pennine Way where you can get a drink. There is also a youth

Border stone at Carter Bar.

hostel and a campsite, but as soon as I heard that the landlord allows walkers to camp in his paddock, there seemed little point in going anywhere else. Later on, I swapped stories with a couple who had bed and breakfasted the entire length of the Pennine Way – the Byrness Hotel being their last stop. Having successfully negotiated over two hundred miles from Edale they were justly confident about the remaining twenty-seven miles to Kirk Yetholm. My own tally was by that stage approaching the seven hundred mark and, as I listened with interest to the highlights of their adventure (which included getting bogged down on Black Hill), I sensed the mixture of satisfaction and sadness in their emotion and reflected that, while *their* journey was drawing to a close, the Pennine Way, for me, had been just one

CHAPTER 10: HADRIAN'S WALL – CARTER BAR

part of something rather larger. I knew that I had all but walked the very length of England and with another country to go, I wondered how I would feel if ever I got to John o' Groats, and in what shape my emotions would be. I suddenly felt very tired and, rather than disgracing myself by dropping off my bar stool or something, I retired to the tent.

The morning was cool and grey. I left around seven to some kind words of encouragement from the landlord, who had risen early to start making breakfasts. I struck out directly for the Scottish border, which I came to, some five miles along, at a point known as Carter Bar.

CHAPTER 11

Carter Bar – Innerleithen

IN WHICH
...an Englishman, taken for a Frenchman, becomes a Scottish prince for the night.

At the border, as I stood by the large monolith admiring wide and wild views across the Cheviots, two notable things happened. The first was extraordinary and concerned a young woman who had stopped her car in the purpose-built lay-by. She approached, got me to turn around so that she could read my sign, and, having fetched some coins from the ashtray of her car, started saying lots of things like "I think what you're doing is marvellous! This must be a special moment for you. You must be very fit ..." And then, as if all that hadn't embarrassed me enough, "I could give you a hug!"

"You can if you like." The words had left my lips before I had allowed myself time to think and we duly embraced. It was a most un-English thing to do and yet she was English, too. I suppose the romance of the setting might have had something to do with it, but I was baffled nonetheless. By the manner that she had stretched, sniffed the air and spun around to take in the panorama, it was clear that this was no mundane commuter run. She was on an adventure herself, heading south in the early morning and, while millions up and down the country lay in bed, in that place she met me.

People's lives intersect. There are those around us of whom we see lots, family and friends, people at work and so forth, there are those whom we might recognise – perhaps the postman, someone on the railway platform, at the local, or in the supermarket where we shop, but there are also many people we encounter just once in our lives,

CHAPTER 11: CARTER BAR – INNERLEITHEN

particularly if we go anywhere. Consider someone in the next seat aboard an aeroplane or the cashier at a motorway service station: in the normal run of events, once the transaction is complete, we have no further dealings, and we continue our separate lives more or less unaffected. Society gives rise to any number of such chance meetings, yet I could contemplate that, having extracted myself from society, very nearly all my encounters were of this type. The girl returned to her car, I to my rucksack, propped up against the border stone. Unlike the family which I had repeatedly bumped into on the path from Macclesfield, there would be no second meeting. A few words, a small donation to charity, and an embrace: our transaction was complete.

The other thing to happen there was that it started to rain – hard.

I did just double-check that it was also raining in England and that this wasn't the start of some spooky jinx and reflected how lucky I had been with the weather. Apart from the one thorough soaking that day between Glossop and Huddersfield and the flash floods in Gloucestershire – which I dodged reasonably well – my main problem had been with it being too hot, but as I set off again it seemed as if Scotland was set to make up for it!

Along an exposed road running north-west I walked eleven miles to the village of Bonchester Bridge with only one stop, to remove a stone from my boot. This didn't happen very often but, if it had done, I might have known better than to try to take a boot off standing on one leg. I didn't sit down simply because the grass was wet and my shorts weren't shielded by my cagoule. I overbalanced and toppled backwards under the weight of the rucksack like a felled pine somewhere in the Kielder Forest and bumped my head on a post. It was my turn to feel silly... but there was no lasting harm done and there was nobody there to see it!

Hungry and in need of a rest, I stopped at The Horse and Hound, which I recommend highly for its friendly atmosphere and absolutely excellent beef stew. I could have whiled away more time in comfort there at Bonchester Bridge, but I had in mind the possibility of reaching Selkirk that day. A staffroom colleague had offered, on her mother-in-law's behalf, a bed for the night when she learned that I planned to be walking through. Back in June we had made tentative arrangements and I resolved to try to make contact and see if the offer still stood – which it did. With nearly twenty miles still to go, I didn't dally.

In hindsight, I probably should have given my lunch a little longer to settle, because I came over very dizzy near the top of the long ascent out of Bonchester when I stopped to examine an exceptionally large and colourful thistle growing in the hedgerow. I reeled for a moment and sat down thinking to myself 'steady the Buffs'.[34]

Rallying, I took a minute or so to look again at the thistles, proud emblems of Scotland. I picked a smaller and less prickly-looking specimen and continued along the way, at a rather gentler pace, and by mid-afternoon had reached a place overlooking the town of Hawick. The rain had abated and I paused again, this time to study the maps and to review my options. I needed a direct route more or less due north and, in the absence of clear footpaths, I reluctantly plumped for the main A7. Before that, there was the immediate and obvious obstacle of the River Teviot, which I crossed by a charming high stone bridge, about a mile to the east of the town. The water was dark and deep. I leant over the wall and dropped a pebble. One cat-er-pil-lar PLOP. A couple with a pushchair containing a small child were also on the bridge, holidaymakers from Yorkshire. The child's father came and stood at my shoulder and also plopped a pebble.

"Do you think its deep enough to jump in?" I had no intention of so doing, but asked his opinion all the same.

---

[34] The Buffs (The Royal East Kent) was an infantry regiment of the British Army. "Steady the Buffs!" was a mocking call used by a rival regiment, the 21st Fusiliers.

CHAPTER 11: CARTER BAR – INNERLEITHEN

"Some lads from the campsite were jumping in yesterday. Gypsies," he replied. I said I wished that I had been there to see it, and enquired if he were tempted.

"Not bloody likely!"

Another one-off encounter had passed but, as you will learn, I had cause to remember the conversation and the image it captured.

If that fellow's accent and intonation had given away his upbringing in Leeds or thereabouts, I was not so certain about the next people I met, nor (not surprisingly) were they of me.

They were a bunch of local youngsters in the sleepy and charmingly named village of Appletreehall, to the north-east of Hawick. Out on their bikes, they had first buzzed past me, then doubled back, to challenge me. Standing astride their bikes, one of them, a girl, I think – but I wasn't certain – said something that sounded like 'Bonjour'.

I nodded. Another ventured the same, although less distinct.

"Bonjour." Some kind of joke I imagined, and I decided to play along.

"Bonjour!" I replied loudly. "Comment ça va?"

From the giggles and the ensuing awkward silence, I took it that they had either been rumbled or bamboozled. They cycled a few yards up the road in the direction that I was heading. Out of earshot they consulted. I carried on walking and, as I approached, there came a question:

"'r' you French?"

"Moi? Non. Je suis anglais." I was having a good time, but they, too, seemed to be enjoying the joke.

I translated and inevitably was informed.

"We tho' you were French."

Now, however bad my French accent was and however much difficulty they experienced in making sense of it, I was really struggling with *their* accents. Their words sounded to me like a broad mixture of Geordie and Glaswegian, and whatever they uttered I found myself saying 'Pardon?' 'Sorry?' or 'You what?' Even in rural Somerset I had found things easier!

They accompanied me to a phone box, where I phoned ahead with my E.T.A. at Selkirk. The only coin I had was a one-pound and the telephone's digital display showed that, following my call, there remained a non-returnable credit. I leant out of the kiosk and asked the youngsters:

"Does anybody want to make a call? There's 88p credit here."

Pressing the 'follow-on call' button, they made a string of nuisance calls to mums or friends, just for the sake of it.

"Hello. It's me ... yeah, bye now," was typical.

The children knew of John o' Groats but wanted to know where Land's End was.

"Cornwall. At the tip of England."

"That's near Devon," one commented. "Me aun'ie lives i' Devon."

The youngsters dismissed as completely impossible my assertion that I had already walked from there. They would no more have believed me if I had said I had walked from Paris. It might have seemed more plausible that I had beamed down from another planet!

My rucksack was against the phone box. This was no TARDIS[35] and it's impossible to be inside a phone box wearing a large pack. I did try it once or twice, but you can't get far enough away from the phone itself to use it. My young companions were curious and I asked one if he wanted to try it on. Then they all wanted to try it. We laughed as they clowned around and stumbled about under its weight... and I only put a stop to the game when one of their number, who was well developed and definitely a female, got into a spot of bother with the elasticated chest straps which hold the upper part of the load close to the body. The others barracked and lambasted:

---

[35] The acronym TARDIS is 'Time and relative dimension in space'. It refers to the expanding time-travel machine in BBC Television's long-running sci-fi adventure series *Doctor Who*.

CHAPTER 11: CARTER BAR – INNERLEITHEN

"Your titties in the way!" I did my best to spare her blushes.

The group cycled with me right out of the village, as far as the main road, and several minutes after we'd said our goodbyes, I happened to look back as I reached the brow of the first hill. They were still waiting at the junction, watching me. I raised my arm and waved... and they all waved back.

That section of the A7 was not as busy as I had expected. There are wide verges on either side which, although uneven, provided a degree of comfort whenever a fast car or lorry came by. The morning's rain clouds had cleared completely, and I was able to enjoy the rolling views of the country in all directions.

Where coniferous planting comes close to the road, I looked straight ahead, but not grimly. I had no desire to study the pine trees: after all, I had seen one or two in the Kielder Forest. Instead, I slipped into metrical march mode and ate up a few miles in a contented state, thinking nothing in particular – if anything, contemplating the 'A7-ness' of the road. By this, I mean that, since setting off from Land's End, I had been conscious of road numbers. You may know that there is a certain logicality to road numbering in Britain. It starts from London with the A1 which heads north. The roads in Cornwall and Devon relate to the A3 with numbers beginning with 3. As I made progress up country, I came to roads beginning with 4, 5, 6 and here 7. The road to John o' Groats is the A9. It was a way of marking off progress... and it kept this particular simple-minded fellow happy for hours until that evening I came to the outskirts of Selkirk.

I needed provisions. It being a Saturday, I thought it as well to find a shop that evening rather than gamble the following morning, so I carried on, down into the town centre.

I had been to Selkirk a few times before and roughly knew my way around. In the main square which, having been washed by the earlier rain, was looking clean and attractive, there was plenty of activity.

The townsfolk were enjoying the evening. I was propositioned, by the floodlit statue of Sir Walter Scott.

"Hey, Jimmy!" (I knew he meant me.) "How d'you like to caddy for me? I need someone to caddy tomorrow."

There was general laughter. The heckler was one of a number of men changing pubs. I think they had been watching football. Apart from having other plans, the prospect of an additional hot walk, with no net mileage gain, carrying someone else's kit, did not really appeal. Even if he had been serious, I would still have declined. I found a store and then doubled back up the hill to a road I had passed earlier. This time, I walked up it and knocked at number twenty.

I must have been spotted approaching, for the door opened immediately. My hostess had a manner about her which made me feel comfortable right away. I was greeted not as an old friend, nor as a total stranger, but warmly all the same. I could leave my boots in the porch to air, if I wanted to: wasn't it a warm evening and how did I take my tea?

Having nearly sat on the cat, I drank the tea while Mrs Robertson made easy conversation. It wasn't long before she mentioned the magic word "bath". Duly scrubbed and having eaten a meal fit for a Scottish prince, we drank more tea and talked of many things until late.

People who run the marathon speak of 'hitting the wall'. This is a phenomenon related to oxygen debt in the body which typically results in any kind of agony at around seventeen miles. My own 'wall' took a different form and I reached it just before midnight when mid-conversation, I realised that I could only remain awake for a few more moments. Making a dart for bed, I tumbled up the stairs and assumed a horizontal position with only seconds to spare.

It was a fine morning in Selkirk, made all the finer by what could only be termed a 'full Scottish breakfast' to match the feast laid on for me the previous evening. At the bottom of the town, I dazzled myself for a while looking at the sun's reflection sparkling in Ettrick Water

CHAPTER 11: CARTER BAR – INNERLEITHEN

and then followed the riverbank for a few miles until I came across a group of trainee canoeists near the youth hostel at Broadmeadows. Considering the heat of the day, the water must have been very cold and they must have been in it on capsizing drill for a long time, for they were shivering and blue with cold. Only the instructor, shouting commands and standing tall and proud with water up to his waist, seemed immune to the chill. People do seek their enjoyment in the most peculiar ways, I thought, as under the midday sun, this particular Englishman (carrying something rather like a large sack of potatoes) began an ascent of around 1800 feet, to join the Southern Upland Way.

This 202-mile walkers' classic links Cockburnspath on the east coast, near Dunbar, with Portpatrick on the west coast. Although, not surprisingly, much of the path goes east-west, and although I really *ought* to have been heading south to north, I was nevertheless keen to experience the track first-hand. I recalled the chap I'd met in the Midlands, when I had been dead on my feet at the campsite north of Kidderminster, and how he had sung the praises of the Southern Upland Way. My plan was to follow it over the hills and across Minch Moor.

There were quite a few people walking the way. I guessed it must be popular terrain for ramblers and 'daysackers'.

"This is the place to be!" concurred one, who broke off from her sandwich to say as much when I passed. I even came across a line of inappropriately shod Japanese tourists, who were lost! I told them to follow the 'thistle'-painted waymarkers, etched on wooden posts. I thought about telling them about a giant Wellingtonia which had fallen and was blocking the way down to Broadmeadows, but from the nodding and smiling (and the manner of their original question) I supposed that their English was about as good as my Japanese. Unlike James Bond, I do not have a double first in Oriental languages from Cambridge ... so I smiled and nodded, too, and pointed.

The views are outstanding on Minch Moor: hills and heather in all directions. I sat for a time, gazing due north, contemplating first the grandeur and sheer beauty of the scene and then, as my eye rested on the point at which sky and distant mountains became indistinguishable in the shimmering haze, the rigours of the challenge ahead. As anyone who has stood, for example, on the summit of Mount Snowdon (when it is not in cloud) knows, one comprehends matters of scale far better at times like these than one does looking out of the kitchen window at a garden fence. With a sigh which, therefore, was partly aesthetic and partly exasperation, I roused myself and set out, focussing on the more immediate objective of reaching Traquair Forest, which offered the prospect of a little shade.

I came to the forest along the historic drove road used by many a hunting monarch and fleeing Royalist. It descends to Traquair House, a haunted castle to be sure and, the guide will tell you, the oldest continuously inhabited house in Scotland. I had picked up a sturdy stick on the way down (there were a few million to choose from but, as Henry Ford might have said, I could have had any one I liked, as long as it was pine)[36] because I began to experience a fiery shooting pain in the ball of my left foot. Trying not to look too much of a Charlie, I passed a toiling couple, to whom I gave the assurance that the climb was well worth it, for the views, and then carried on all the way down to Traquair in 'Jake the Peg'[37] fashion.

It seemed unlikely that a bee had got stuck inside my boot, but when I came to the banks of the Tweed, I checked all the same. Finding neither corpse nor sting to account for things, I tried massaging my foot and, with rather greater success, resorted to completely numbing the whole foot by immersion. A few seconds was all it took for me to

---

[36] Henry Ford (1863-1947) was founder of the Ford Motor Company: "Any customer can have a car painted any color that he wants so long as it is black."

[37] Jake the Peg was the three-legged creation of Australian-born entertainer Rolf Harris.

CHAPTER 11: CARTER BAR – INNERLEITHEN

see why the canoeists had looked so cold, but I kept my foot under water for several minutes. Gradually, head-rolling agony eased into mellow anaesthesia. I peered through the water at my foot. The eddying water, coupled with the refraction and the fact that my suntanned legs were a completely different colour from the skin below the sock line, gave an unusual effect. This monster evidently had a crookedly bolted Frankenstein foot!

After the shock therapy, I felt good enough to discard the walking stick and head gently into the town of Innerleithen. Before long, I had found a comfortable armchair in the bar of The Traquair Arms Hotel and had some more cool and dark liquid to peer into. Some while later and feeling rosier, I wandered north through the town. I was low on food and, as most of the shops were shut, I bought a Chinese takeaway.

Years ago, my brother and I used to joke about what we called "the sloth triangle". To complete the sloth triangle (as I admit to having done habitually at that time) it was necessary to visit the Chinese takeaway, the video rental shop and the off-licence, all on the same evening. I suppose, judging from the fact that these types of establishments are frequently situated next door to each other, lots of people must so indulge. The reminder of a lifestyle I no longer wanted was enough, and instead of consuming my chow mein in front of a television set, I munched al fresco, beside the babbling tributary of the Tweed known as Leithen Water.

With no real intention of going very much further that evening, I followed the river a little way out of the town until I came to the golf course, which is really pretty. Perhaps the egg fried rice had given me more energy, or perhaps the springy grass was especially gentle on my sore foot, but I settled back into my stride, pausing only briefly when I met a golfer looking for his lost ball in some light rough. As it happened, I found a ball. It was not his, but I think he played it all the same.

Beyond the golf course, Leithen Water meanders along the bottom of a valley which must have been glaciated at some stage. With good, flat land next to the river, I saw plenty of excellent places to camp. Unfortunately I was not the only one to have spotted such opportunities, for in every place where it was possible to pull off the road, a caravan or two had done just that, to take up semi-permanent occupancy. For another two hours I walked past rocky places and places with caravans. Eventually, and a good deal higher in the valley, there were fewer caravans, some tents and more space. Wire dustbins had been provided.

"Is this free camping?" I asked a man who, with a crowbar, was poking at his campfire.

"Just about the only place left in Scotland!" His reply seemed ample justification for me to find a spot, at a discreet distance, on which to put up my tent.

CHAPTER 12

Innerleithen – Edinburgh

IN WHICH
...through fog and the Heart of Midlothian, I walk a Royal Mile before learning something of Auld Reekie's darker side.

Thick fog filled the valley when I peeped out early in the morning. Before packing up, I knelt at the river's edge and bravely plunged my whole head under the water for at least a tenth of a second, and shook dry like a dog. Fully awakened, I checked the map. To the north, the Moorfoot Hills were now the only significant natural barrier between me and Edinburgh.

Once the fog lifted from the 2137-foot summit known as Blackhope Scar, I felt sure there would be good views not only of the Pentland Hills to the west, but also of the Scottish capital and its distinctive geography. I could not see Blackhope Scar, nor indeed anything very much beyond the end of my nose, but took a compass bearing and the view that 'upwards' would probably get me to where I wanted to be.

Two or three times I nearly jumped out of my skin having disturbed grouse that were nesting in the heather. As they fly off, grouse shriek a high-pitched gobble which echoes around the hills. Surely amongst nature's great panickers, their panic is not without reason, for perhaps these birds know to fear the sound and sight of man, treading through their habitat at dawn. My 'first grouse' in a manner of speaking, was before seven in the morning. Coincidentally, this was also the month of August... and the date was 'The Glorious Twelfth'![38]

---

[38] 'The Glorious 12th' is August the 12th, the first day of the 121-day open shooting season for red grouse.

I certainly didn't want to attract the attentions, nor fall under the sights, of a party of trigger-happy, sensation-seeking, fee-paying businessmen with a view to an early kill. Hunting is an important part of the Scottish rural economy, although this branch of tourism and the race to have unhung grouse on the menu by lunchtime in London, seemed to me as crazy as those people who make helicopter drops with crates of 'Beaujolais Nouveau' in November of each year.

I heard no gunfire nor saw anybody at all on that hill, but I did meet a rabbit who, unlike others of his type, and the grouse, did not take to flight. The rabbit was badly injured, with one leg hanging by a sinew. The animal was incapable of any movement save twitching. Possibly shot, he may even have limped up from the road but, at that height, I thought it more likely that there had been an earlier, unfinished encounter with a large bird of prey. He had no chance whatever and, after a moment's deliberation (which I'm sure was more painful for him than it was for me) I took action, on the boulder-strewn hillside, to ensure the little creature twitched no more.

It was every bit as misty and murky at the top, and I had to imagine the views of Arthur's Seat and the Firth of Forth. Even so, the image kept me going as I crossed into Midlothian. Following an easy track where the heather was not growing, I tramped north-east through more fog and over another feature, Torfichen Hill, before returning to the level of the road, which was lined with snow poles.

Up quite a steep gradient, coming very slowly towards me out of the gloom appeared a cyclist, wild and woolly. He stopped to say hello (people don't do that where I come from) and we spoke for long enough for him to get his breath back. He was a Russian sailor docked at Newcastle, who was making the most of his shore leave. Like me, he was fed up with the fog. He wished each other well and continued in our separate directions.

I kept to the road on the way down and disturbed no more grouse, but I did catch sight of pheasant and partridge of which any poulterer

CHAPTER 12: INNERLEITHEN – EDINBURGH

would have been proud. In about two hours there passed only one vehicle, a coachload of sightseers who had given up trying to see anything in the fog and had a video on! Perhaps it was Brigadoon.[39]

With the hills behind me, I made good time and came at around midday to the settlement of Middleton, Midlothian. At the centre of this place is a limestone quarrying plant, from whence came the disquieting shudder of deep blasting, together with grinding and groaning of heavy plant.

I would not like to live in Middleton, not so much on account of the noise, which I'm certain you would get used to in the same way that millions living by busy roads learn to cut out the sound of motorways and HGVs, or like schoolteachers, for that matter, who become immune to other forms of sound pollution – but because the whole area was covered in a thick layer of limy dust and the nearer that I got to the gates of the plant, the greyer everything became. Although local gardeners might have other problems, I thought, at least they wouldn't have to deal with acidic soils.

I came to the A7 at that point, and I crossed it, at a gallop, and made for the town of Gorebridge, where I had some lunch and spent some time in the library, looking up such things as ling and bell heather, merlins, eagles, grouse and partridge. I had no need to study the maps for, from that point, all roads seemed to go to Edinburgh. I recall the librarian, a jolly fellow and one of those razor-sharp types who can make two or three jokes per sentence:

"So you've not got far to go, then" (he had seen my rucksack sign). "Just to the end of the road!"

The fog had turned into what I have heard described as mizzle, but it was not cold. I headed towards the city centre along pavemented streets, stopping only when heavier rain forced me into The Liberton

---

[39] *Brigadoon* (MGM, 1954) is the film from Lerner and Loewe's musical about two Americans who get lost in Scottish mist while on a hunting trip.

Inn. I sat down by the window with my drink and thumbed through some papers, minding my own business, but was joined before long by an old man who had worked out a way of carrying beer and walking on two crutches. He didn't spill a drop as he eased himself down beside me. I wondered whether I had taken *his* seat… but he reassured me.

"You're all right." He savoured a sip or two and continued in a manner more of a statement than a question.

"You'd be here for the Tattoo."

I didn't give him the full story but told him that I was just passing through, and then fired one of my own:

"Are you from around here?" I knew the answer, but had a feeling that he had a story or two to tell.

"Lived here all my life."

"All your life so far, don't you mean?"

He laughed bronchitically and said that, after eighty-two years, he had no intention of moving. He told me that he had been drinking at that pub since he was a boy. I presumed not all of the time, although I couldn't help noticing that his eyes were very deeply set and his nose was very red. He went on to tell me something about where we were, and it turned out that not everyone was welcome there. While it would be all right for me to come in, order a pint and sit by the window reading a copy of Walter Scott's *The Heart of Midlothian*, it would certainly not be tolerated were I to come in wearing the replica kit of the football club similarly named, for this was a 'Hibs' pub and there is fierce rivalry between fans of 'Hibs' and 'Hearts'. In fact the Easter Street ground, home of Hibernian football, was just a few minutes away from where we were. It would be just as unwise, I learned, to try crossing the threshold of The Tynecastle Arms wearing a Hibs rosette. I have been in the Catholic quarter of Glasgow on match day and I knew what he was talking about. The atmosphere is frightening, even tribal. Surprisingly, he revealed, he himself was the

CHAPTER 12: INNERLEITHEN – EDINBURGH

exception, a Hearts fan all his life, granted access to The Liberton on account of his seniority and loyal patronage. I decided not to mention that I supported Portsmouth!

I continued my approach to the city centre from the south and from the east, so I presumed that the inhabitants of the houses in rows by which I splashed would also have allegiance to Hibernian… Although I saw no evidence of any football war. My mind was on conflict of a historical kind, such as the capture of the castle from the English by Robert the Bruce in 1313 or the firing of Mons Meg, the massive cannon by the castle chapel's door into which my father had once loaded me, for a photograph. (It does not fire anymore because it burst whilst firing a salute to Charles II in 1680 but, at one time, it could blast a stone shot the weight of a rugby scrum a mile and a half across the city!)

In its long history, the castle may well have looked down upon many a good fight, but on the day that my long march through England and the Scottish Borders came to an end, a castle lookout wouldn't have been able to see anything in the fog and rain. If an invading army could have approached unseen, then one man beneath a rucksack and cagoule certainly went unnoticed in the midst of swelling crowds of tourists and visitors to the Edinburgh Festival and Military Tattoo.

I passed dozens of curry restaurants and balti houses locked in competition for business and offering tempting deals like 'eat as much as you can for £5.95. Bring your own drinks'. As a great enthusiast of spicy food with an extra-large appetite, I felt that I was capable of surprising the restaurateur, had I taken the advert literally, but I took the mature and restrained option of seeking out delights of a different nature in the ancient capital. I wanted to make at least one of my miles a 'Royal' one, so I made for Holyroodhouse at the foot of Canongate. The palace, associated with the tragic history of the Stuarts, looked grim and ghostly against the dark crags which disappeared into the mist. I turned my back on the gates and paced up towards the High Street.

There were thousands of people out in the rain, wandering around. A band of street entertainers, including a fire-eater and some barefooted dancing girls had attracted a large group of onlookers outside the museum where once lived John Knox, fiery Calvinist and Minister at St Giles. I, too, paused for a while to try to make sense of it all.

The cathedral itself dominates the High Street. There also I stopped to see the crown-shaped steeple tops, but by then the thousands had become hundreds of thousands and police were enforcing a blockade: I was not allowed to go further because of the Tattoo, and so doubled back and cut down one of the narrow 'wynds' to climb down to a lower level.

Unlike most cities in Britain, Edinburgh did not grow up along a river valley. Its startling physical geography of plateaux, cliffs and canyons is exaggerated by the height of the old tenements. I did not count the number of steps down to the level of Waverley Station but here, too, there were more than thirty-nine! I lingered neither at the station nor at the Scott Monument... as there seemed little point in climbing the Gothic spire, famed for its 287 steps, given the visibility at the time. It was probably closed anyway.

I walked the length of Princes Street, on the side of the gardens, which held more attraction to me than the department stores and burger bars on the other side, and phoned home.

"Hello. I'm in Edinburgh!"

My exploration of the capital continued with a visit to Rose Street, in which every other house is a public one. As students, we used to refer to the 'Topsham Ten', a pub crawl in that village on the Exe Estuary. I never did visit all ten in one evening; in those days it seemed like too much walking and we found it difficult to think of a good reason to move on from places like The Bridge or The

CHAPTER 12: INNERLEITHEN – EDINBURGH

Passage. Here, in Rose Street, there were more pubs and less distance. I was not in the mood for sideways walking and spending the night in a cell, even if the old prison had been demolished in 1817, so I chose just one to visit, the Rose Street Brewery, where they sell 'ninety shilling', which is very strong. I offer the following observation on the subject of beer and monetary inflation: the ninety shilling I drank that evening is so-named because that, in the 19th century, was the price of a hogshead of the ale. A hogshead is fifty-four gallons, which is two hundred and fifty litres, or four hundred and thirty-two pints. These days, ninety shillings (a shilling being one twentieth of a pound) would probably buy not four hundred and thirty-two pints, but just one. Ah well!

An Irish folk band was playing live inside. "And why not?" I said to myself, meaning that there was no reason why they had to be a Scottish folk group, even if the tartan is laid on a bit thick for the coachloads of tourists in other parts of town.

I listened to a couple of songs, even joining in the chorus, but then the frontman announced:

"We're going to take a break now..." So I moved on, but took with me a strain of melody. An idea had come to me. I would write a song to sing with the children back at school. I shuffled along the pavement juggling words in my head and a couple of lines began to fit into place:

"'Tis of a fine young teacher lad the story I will tell:
He worked at the school that you know very well ...."

This would be the start of the 'Land's End to John o' Groats Ballad' – and I had the last bit, too:

"No more, no more, no more, me boys,
If ever I get to John o' Groats, I'll never walk no more!"

Resolving to give the lyric more thought, I continued on my way. Having been propositioned (not golf, this time) I beat a hasty retreat into respectable George Street where banks and offices make use of the fine Georgian architecture, and from there on into Charlotte Square, the elegant north side of which was designed by Robert Adam.[40]

I continued northwards with the idea that eventually I was certain to come to the Firth of Forth. I had details of a camping site on the Firth. Perhaps I could get in there.

Several times I was reminded of what an unpleasant sight it is to see people who are really drunk, and congratulated myself for making my visit to Rose Street comparatively brief. I was in much better shape than some I saw, shoving each other or spewing on the pavement. As it transpired, I would need my wits about me.

A group of lads came around a corner, saw me, and started running at me. Was I a soft target for a mugging? I wondered. Unable to run away I thought of how best to react and decided to carry on. I was jostled but neither thumped nor robbed which was a relief, for the whole matter was very threatening. Little, if anything, was said. Perhaps the sight of my big bots had made a difference, or the fact that my giant rucksack added height and width to my figure. Perhaps it was that these youths got their kicks from merely scaring the living daylights out of people. Not for the first time, I remembered the words of Henry on Dartmoor, when I had asked pessimistically what the worst thing that could happen to me was.

"You might have your stuff stolen," he had warned. So far, I had avoided a catalogue of perils from mad dogs to the tipper lorry on the point of tipping over, but now, in north Edinburgh, I was in a rough area, after dark, miles from home... and it was raining. 'Survival' seemed to be the name of the game.

As you will gather, I did survive and, having passed any number of dark premises bound up in barbed and razor wire, I located the campsite. 'No vacancies', read a stark sign on the door of the rather

---

[40] Robert Adam (1728-92): neoclassical architect, interior designer and furniture designer whose work profoundly influenced design on both sides of the Atlantic.

CHAPTER 12: INNERLEITHEN – EDINBURGH

plush reception building. An automated barrier was down and staying down. The whole campsite, too, was surrounded with security fencing and it looked very much like there was 'no room at the inn'. A bedraggled cyclist joined me by the sign. We ducked under the barrier and passing several signs of the 'NO UNAUTHORISED ENTRY' type, entered the camp.

Bona fide tenters all displayed large, reflective numbers, no doubt so that a warden with a torch could easily see if there were any interlopers. The cyclist went one way, I another, each looking for a shady and inconspicuous spot where we might be able to pitch, undetected. Every spot seemed to have been taken on either side of the narrow service track, but right in the corner I spotted a gap. There was a reason why no tent stood there. The plot was roped off and closer examination revealed that the area had just been returfed. I decided to do the proprietors a favour and help to flatten down the turf, so I stepped over the rope and, as quickly and quietly as I could, erected the tent.

CHAPTER 13

Edinburgh – Loch Leven

IN WHICH
*...in a new kingdom, musicians, a football hero, "the press"
and a child-catcher make for an unusual schoolday.*

The next day was an important one, for I would be completing a school's liaison on the other side of the Firth in the village of Aberdour, after which my own school was named.

I was due to meet the headmistress and some of the Scottish Aberdorians at two o'clock, so I made an early start. It had stopped raining but the fog hadn't cleared. As I strolled briskly along the shore towards Cramond I peered out over the Forth. In the gloom, I could just make out Cramond Island at the end of an eerie line of a hundred or so concrete posts along the edge of a causeway, which is exposed at low tide. Beyond the island, right over on the other side of the Firth, and completely invisible, was Aberdour.

I met a fisherman (who told me about the causeway) and a couple of festival revellers, who had evidently strayed out of town sometime during the night and were making their way back up into the city. Before long, I came to the mouth of the River Almond, which flows into the Firth of Forth. I had heard that there was a foot ferry across the Almond and was wondering if it might be considered cheating to use it, as I had thus far walked every step from Land's End. On the other hand, I thought to myself, it was a lengthy detour inland to Cramond Bridge. I was undecided, and made a couple of time/distance calculations when, as so often during those weeks, circumstances ultimately gave me no choice. In this case, I was about two hours too early for the ferryman, so I saved myself the fare, and the anxiety, and

CHAPTER 13: EDINBURGH – LOCH LEVEN

Crammond.

The River Almond.

pressed on inland, due south, for the first time since wandering around Chipping Sodbury.

With its weeping willows, weirs and waterfalls, the Almond, in its last couple of miles, is a pretty river. The authorities in Midlothian have recognised this and have created a recreational walkway which shadows the east bank. I was feeling mildly frustrated because it's the sort of path which goes up sixty-one steps then down fifty-nine then up and down some more – difficult in a wheelchair, I imagined. I crossed the old bridge on which, in the year 1436, James I had been warned not to continue his journey: he ignored the advice and was duly murdered shortly after his arrival at Perth. There was no soothsayer waiting for me, so I continued and was rewarded with my first clear view of the two mighty constructions leading to the Kingdom of Fife.

At Queensferry, right under the colossal iron girders of the railway bridge, I was lining up a photo when a coach party of tourists pulled up. I eavesdropped on what the guide was explaining, but was challenged by a pair of workmen who were painting the railings right by where the coach-trippers had gathered around their guide.

"Are you really going all the way to Groats?"

It was a familiar question by then. We laughed, agreed that I was mad and then witnessed the inevitable as several preoccupied tourists leant up against the painty railings, in spite of my attempts at intervention.

There is a safe and gantried walkway across the road bridge along which you can walk or cycle. It's nearly two miles long, so I had about forty minutes in which to contemplate the scale and situation of the bridges. I was astonished by how much the structure of the road bridge vibrates as the stream of traffic thunders across. I told myself that it is meant to move, but there were other things to alarm the faint-hearted, not least its height above the water. The vessels passing below looked like toy boats in a giant bath which also contained dozens of huge, dead jellyfish and, halfway along, corrosion engineers were pumping

CHAPTER 13: EDINBURGH – LOCH LEVEN

high-pressure steam through hissing and groaning pipes, presumably because the bridge is rusting away.

The views downstream to the awesome railway bridge easily suppressed any latent vertigo or aquaphobia. I knew that this feat of Victorian engineering has carried many thousands of holidaymakers, including our school's first head teacher, to resorts like Aberdour. I looked along the coast and then back across the road bridge. Through the fog, I hadn't expected to see Edinburgh Castle or King Arthur's Seat, but I couldn't even see the other end of the bridge! I was relieved to give my knees a rest after their vibro-massage therapy on the wobbling gantry; they felt rather like Tom's head after that unfortunate cartoon cat jams it in a tin bucket which Jerry then wallops with a giant mallet.

At Inverkeithing I paused at a sandwich bar for a roll which was garnished with lots of strong raw onion. Hot and sweaty, I wondered what sort of impression I would make meeting the others in a couple of hours. I resolved to scrub up a bit and brush my teeth if I came to a pub along the way. Then I saw a signpost reading: 'Aberdour 6' and on the other side of the huge Shell Oil depot and refinery another: 'Aberdour 3'. Thinking of football scores and remembering a sign on the M27 I used to drive past occasionally (on the way to Fratton Park[41]) which reads: 'Southampton 2, Portsmouth 19' and wondering if there are signs which say things like 'Manchester 1 Liverpool 40', I finally passed one which said: 'Welcome to Aberdour, please drive carefully'.

The outskirts of Aberdour are nothing special. There is a row of 1930s semi-detached houses, although some have beautifully kept gardens. In one of these was a lady, dead-heading her roses.

I asked if she could give directions to Hawkcraig Road; she could, but she wanted to know what was going on there. I explained that I

---

[41] Fratton Park is the home of Portsmouth Football Club, and has been since the club was founded in 1898. Located on Portsea Island, it is the only stadium of a British professional football club not on mainland Britain.

taught at a school called Aberdour, that I had walked from Cornwall, that I was meeting the headmistress, and that the press would be there.

"You had better come in then, you look thirsty." It was something of a non sequitur but I had a little time and the thought of cool running water was tempting.

"Thank you, I will!"

To her sophisticated teenage daughter, who was playing the flute, she introduced me as: "a hitch-hiker who's going to school".

I was on about my fourth tumbler of Forth water and chatting easily to the young musician when I became aware of my kind-hearted host's chief glory: she was an administrator and organiser of people *par excellence*. She was busily making around thirty phone calls to families in the village with the idea of swelling numbers at my reception. Her main persuasive point was that "the press" were coming. Every so often, she would put her head around the door and announce with a gleeful smile, like some maniacal child catcher:

"I've got another one!"

With about five minutes to spare, I was escorted through the streets of Wester Aberdour, as that part of the town is known, rounding up children as surely as did the Pied Piper, although some Year Six-ish boys did prefer to continue swimming and rock-pooling. I didn't blame then, for it was sultry hot and the sun was just about breaking through – besides which, Aberdour's West Sands are, I have no doubt, a great place to while away the long summer holidays.

Aberdour means 'mouth of the Dour'. The Dour Burn is the stream which runs into the narrow harbour, dividing the village in two. In the harbour were dozens of small craft, the majority of which were sailing dinghies moored to an old stone pier. We crossed the Burn and climbed up a steep track known as 'Donkey Brae'. Along that way, I learned, a donkey is still driven, at festival time, to re-enact the history of supplying Aberdour Castle, which is at the top of the hill.

CHAPTER 13: EDINBURGH – LOCH LEVEN

Aberdour School is midway between the harbour and the castle, but it is certainly not as ancient as either. My reception committee, which included children, staff and 'the janitor', were waiting inside the concrete entrance area. A reporter from the Dunfermline Press arrived, whom I was pleased to see, because he had with him the presentation shield from our school which my wife had posted, rather than see me carry all the way from Land's End. We all posed for a photocall and then spent a while cementing the inter-school liaison. The children disappeared and before long so did everyone else. I had reached my objective and I knew that this had secured a good deal of sponsorship money, but I was not especially into self-congratulation at that time... I had more pressing things on my mind: I wanted to explore the rest of the village; I quite badly wanted a drink, I had to sort out somewhere to stay and, having covered about 680 miles, I knew that it was still another 320 to my ultimate destination.

It seemed a good idea to visit the castle, so I strolled up the road from the school. Partly in ruins, Aberdour Castle has a long history. Work started around 1200 on instructions from the de Mortimer family. I was told that the stretch of water between the harbour and Inchcolm Island, two miles into the Firth, is known as 'Mortimer's Deep', after the body of one John Mortimer was offloaded by monks in a rowing boat returning to Inchcolm Abbey – apparently Mortimer had asked to be buried on the island.

Over the centuries, Aberdour Castle passed into and out of the hands of a number of eminent Scottish families. Its heyday, from what I can gather, was probably during the 16th century, when Robert, Earl of Morton, had extensive improvements carried out. A couple of hundred years passed before a massive fire caused it to be abandoned (in favour of neighbouring Aberdour House) as a principal residence... and another couple of hundred or so years passed before Historic Scotland took over its care and maintenance. The striking feature of the castle gardens is the immaculate grass, which gave the

Aberdour.

Aberdour Castle.

impression that only the head gardener (or perhaps one of his most trusted assistants with a minimum of sixty years' experience) would ever be permitted to set foot upon it at all. To my surprise, it turned out that this is not the case, as receptions are frequently held in the grounds, presumably at a premium.

Near the 16th-century dovecote, which is shaped like a giant beehive, I did meet an assistant gardener of considerable experience. I told him that the school badge on the shield I had just presented shows the beehive.

"How do you get the grass to look so good?" I asked, innocently enough.

"Well, first you take out all the stones, rake, roll and seed."

I had an idea where his party piece was leading.

"Then what?"

"You keep the seedlings watered and give the first cut when they're about three inches tall."

"Yes."

"Then you cut and roll regularly in the growing season until it comes up like this."

I was sure now that I was 'being had' but played along all the same.

"And how long would that be for?"

"Ooh about a hundred and fifty years!"

My next stop was at St. Fillan's Church, which is Norman, although it had to be restored in the 1920s. Apparently, after the battle of Bannockburn in 1348, Robert the Bruce gave thanks in the church. There is some fine stained glass, and a Bible dated 1628. I enjoyed the serenity of the atmosphere and the cool of the shade!

From there, I headed along Main Street towards the railway station, which regularly wins prizes for having the greatest number of tubs and hanging baskets …or something like that. You will have guessed that I am no great fan of commuting, but I imagine the thirty-minute run from Aberdour, over the bridge and into Edinburgh Princes Street, is a good deal better for the spirit than other journeys to work that I could think of!

I left the village along a narrow lane to the north that climbs to a place known as Goat Quarry. I had been warned about the lorries turning out of the quarry but even so, when a heavily laden vehicle did just that, I had to make a snap decision between flattening myself against the hedgerow, or being flattened into the tarmac... and then it happened again!

After the lorries, I saw no more traffic until, some while later, when I was sitting on a grassy bank at the top of the hill. I was approached, at a pace slower than my usual, by a wobbly cyclist in a dark suit. Drenched in sweat, he sat high on a rickety old bike that looked about fifty years old. Tied to the back was his suitcase, leather and as old as his velocipede. Dumping the bicycle onto the grass beside me in a manner which suggested he had no great love for the contraption, he flopped down alongside it and groaned.

"Hello," I ventured.

"Hallo." (He was German.) "Is there near here an inn?"

"There are pubs back there in Aberdour. It's about four miles. Six kilometres." I held up six fingers. He groaned again, looked down the hill and then the other way, which looked flatter.

"Not hill again!" We laughed and I offered him a slurp from my water bottle, for which he was grateful. "Zank you!"

I checked the map and showed him that we were not far short of Crossgates, where I assured him there would be an inn.

"B and B?" It dawned on me that he wanted somewhere to stay and I apologised for being so slow on the uptake.

"Sorry. I don't know. You might be better off in Dunfermline. Look. Here..." He followed my finger on the map. "It's about four miles. Six kilometres!"

This time, I groaned for him – and he saw the joke.

"I come from Edinburgh," he announced. I nearly said, "Oh no,

CHAPTER 13: EDINBURGH – LOCH LEVEN

you don't!" but stopped myself just in time, saying instead:

"Ah, you've come from Edinburgh on your bike."

"Not my bike. I hire bike."

I was surprised. He must have found somewhere pretty downmarket and been palmed off with the bottom of the range. I felt sorry for him.

"I come for Edinburgh Festival." (That didn't surprise me.) And then he added, "I play jazz music. Trumpet."

"Oh! Good. You're a jazz trumpeter!" I thought for a moment and came up with a few names. "Miles Davis, Dizzy Gillespie, Louis Armstrong."

He nodded reverently and continued to do so as he repeated, "Louis Armstrong."

"Is your trumpet in there?" I pointed to his suitcase. I can recognise trumpet cases and knew that his case was too big – but it was still possible.

"No, I leave it in Edinburgh." I was disappointed. I think an impromptu roadside jamming session, however brief, would have made my day, for I was ready to clap, click, whistle or croon – but it was not to be.

He seemed content to sit and chat, which we continued to do for some time. It was pleasant enough, for the sun had once more made an appearance through the heavy atmosphere but, by and by, I felt the urge to press on and left the fellow sitting there. A couple of minutes later, on a long, downhill stretch, he coasted past me on the road, making a form of salute by stretching both his legs out, away from the pedals. I waved and he did, too, but nearly came to regret it, for it caused him to veer sideways towards a hedge. He recovered the situation and I retain the image of him snaking along that road into the distance.

I learned later that he had stopped at The Coaledge Tavern, where the famous former footballer Alex Smith now does a good line in 'toasties'. Back in the late-60s, he had been the toast of many a

Rangers supporter's glass, as he was their leading goalscorer. Pressing me to a tot of single malt and a number of other goodies to keep me going, this most hospitable of hosts told how the German cyclist had made an impression there, too, before being redirected east into Dunfermline.

Naturally I headed north. Lines of orange sodium lamps had come on over the streets of Cowdenbeath by the time I navigated the outskirts of town, I walked at full speed, for there were more gangs of youths hanging around in areas which seemed to me very depressed. I passed, with some relief, into more open country and continued walking in failing light until I came to Kelty.

By this stage, I was dog-tired and on the lookout for somewhere to tent. Unfortunately, Kelty is not a good place to camp – but I did get an offer of accommodation. It came from another wobbler, this time a pedestrian, whom I overtook, as he crashed from kerb to concrete bus shelter. He was singing, or at least chanting, in a full voice which was saturated in self-pity, over and over again: "That woman ruined me!"

"Hey, Jimmy!" he called after me. I was reluctant to acknowledge, but turned my head a little. There was no one else around.

"Hey, Jimmy!" he repeated, steadying himself against a wall. "D'you need a bed?... I know what it's like to be on the streets...That woman ruined me, you know..."

I lied and said that I had got somewhere to stay, but he persisted, rambling on, and saying that we could have a drink. It was not enough to tempt me and I quickened my step. He called out something like "you take care", before returning to his refrain. "That woman, she ..."

"Shut up!" someone bellowed from an upstairs window, which then slammed shut.

And so it was that I continued through Kelty and out again into open country. At a safe distance from town, I climbed a fence into a field which looked a possible place to camp, but was chased away by the attentions of some aggressive horses who would not leave me or my

CHAPTER 13: EDINBURGH – LOCH LEVEN

rucksack alone. Up the road I was driven away from what seemed to be a campsite by the mad barking of several dogs that must have smelt me as I approached a building with my torch. Under the circumstances, and, even though I had been on my feet for about sixteen hours that day, it seemed best to carry on. My feet seemed to know what to do, so on automatic pilot, I continued for about another mile.

If you have ever walked at night, looked above you at the stars and seen none, because of cloud, you will know that the sky can be pretty black – and yet you will be able to make out the branches of overhanging trees, for they are blacker still. It was like that, as I became aware of a jet-black feature ahead of me – an unexpected lump of high ground. I reached for my head torch, identified Benarty Hill and decided to climb it straight away.

I would not normally recommend midnight climbing expeditions but by the light of my head torch trained immediately ahead of each step, I made the ascent without so much as a trip or turned ankle. At a spot near the 1168' summit and with the torch batteries failing, I pitched tent.

I woke to the sound of traffic on the M90, which I could see below me to the west. The wind must have changed, I thought, and sure enough, the misty, foggy, cloudy air had gone. It was cooler, fresher and clearer and my spirits soared as I looked around. The sun was just up over the Lomond Hills to the east, and to the south I could retrace much of my route of the previous day, although the Firth still seemed to be foggy, but I looked mainly north. At my feet, Loch Leven, complete with castle and island, shimmered under wisps of clearing mist. It made a pretty picture but I looked beyond, to a faint grey line on the horizon, two or three days' walk away. The maps confirmed what I already knew: these were 'grown-up' mountains, 'the big stuff', and I swallowed as I strained my eyes, trying to pick out individual features. My stomach rumbled, too, as if to ask, 'Are you sure?... Oh, and by the way, how about breakfast?'

CHAPTER 14

Loch Leven – Pitlochry

IN WHICH
...though progress through Perthshire is slow, I take heart from the scenery and from another musical encounter. In Scott's "Fair City", I take shelter, before dining with another literary figure.

Packing up the tent, feelings of self-doubt were heightened when I noticed how precariously close I had positioned the tent to a cliff. It was a good thing that I must have been far too tired to take up sleepwalking! In fact, there seemed no safe way down the hill to the north and not wishing to 'backtrack', I edged along the top until I came to a viewpoint and an easy path down to the Loch and the RSPB[42] visitor centre at Vane Farm.

Apparently, there were at least fifty species of bird's nest in the area. For reasons of weight economy, I had chosen not to carry binoculars: at times I was sorry, and so made it my sport just then to spot ornithologists rather than birds. Of the former, I counted several, typically viewing from the warmth and comfort of their parked cars.

The town of Kinross, which lies on the north-west shore of Loch Leven, is well serviced by the M90. As a result, the old road, running parallel, carries only the most local of traffic. At that time of the morning, I can only have been passed by one or two vehicles in the hour that it took me to reach Kinross, so I was able to savour the changing views of the loch, which has been declared a National Nature Reserve, in tranquillity.

---

[42] Royal Society for the Protection of Birds. It was founded in 1889 as The Plumage League.

CHAPTER 14: LOCH LEVEN – PITLOCHRY

A sign beside the road, pointing into a small industrial estate on the outskirts of the town, invited whatever traffic there was to pull in for snacks. I needed no second invitation and easily smelt out the mobile café.

"Would you like haggis as well?" the lady asked. "...And white pudding?" It all seemed too good to be true. My full breakfast, fried before my bulging eyes, set me back no more than would a cup of coffee in London.

"Have you come far?" she asked, flipping bacon and simultaneously cracking an egg with a well-practised hand.

"Pretty far," I replied and I showed her my sign.

"Oh!" she exclaimed and she went on to say how only last week she had a team of firemen stop there, walking the other way.

"Are you sure it was last week?" I checked, wondering in the first place how many teams of firemen there could be who were walking from John o' Groats to Land's End and then, having reassured myself that it must have been the same brigade that I'd seen on their final lap, how on earth they could have got there so quickly!

"Last week ... or was it the week before? No, I think you're right. The week before." That was more like it, I thought but, even so, it was some going: fifty miles a day, I reckoned.

"They were doing it in shifts ..." (I supposed firemen would be used to that) "…you know …relay."

That would have explained it. One or two would walk, I imagined, for a few hours and then crash out in the support vehicle, while fresh crew would take up the challenge, their numbers swollen by local support.

"I'm pleased they made it then," the lady said, wishing me luck as well. "Would you like another coffee?"

Stuffed to the gills, I took my leave and pressed on through Kinross.

Where the road climbs to go over a dismantled railway line and one of the burns which feeds Loch Leven, I was singing part of the ballad and was surprised by a cyclist, who came up behind me on something much better oiled, and far quieter than the German jazzer's squeaky bike. The woman stopped to say hello. Her voice was soft and lilting with a musical quality of its own. She had heard my song and encouraged me to continue. I was embarrassed because people sing in church, at football matches or in the bath, but not generally while walking along the road. Singing whilst cycling can be hazardous and I do not recommend it. Known to certain singers, the troubles of an old lady who swallowed a fly, a spider, a bird, a cat and so on may well have started in such a fashion. To my knowledge, the riddle in that song, 'I don't know why she swallowed a fly', has never before been solved. Is there now one less musical enigma? In any event, and aside from the original blushes, the consequences for me were happier, as I was invited for a cold drink at her house along the road in Minathort.

"I'll get the glasses out," she said, cycling on but not telling me the house number. I supposed that it would be obvious, or else that she would keep a lookout for me. It was obvious, at least as soon as I saw her bicycle leaning against a house in South Street, which is the main thoroughfare. People don't do that either where we live.

Inside, I met her son and cooled down with iced water. I noticed several crucifixes and a figurine of the Virgin Mary, from which it was not hard to guess that they were devout Catholics. We spoke mainly of matters of faith and about the relief of cancer. I do not know if she had a professional occupation but when she spoke there was such confidence and about her such an aura of calm that it struck me she would be perfect in a field such as bereavement counselling. I was sponsored, blessed and waved off.

I headed out of Minathort making for the next range of hills, the Ochils. Not a human soul did I see for about four hours, nor very much evidence of their activity apart from a few curious DayGlo boards

CHAPTER 14: LOCH LEVEN – PITLOCHRY

mounted, with precision, on posts near the Glenfarg Reservoir. Their purpose is still a mystery to me, although I guessed at the time that they may have been left by surveyors or seismologists. My company consisted mainly of rabbits and corn lice. If the rabbits were enjoying a good year – and there were a great many – the corn lice must have outnumbered them by several million to one. Also known in other parts as 'thunderflies', these tiny black insects were everywhere. Each time I mopped my brow, ten or twenty would be converted to smudges. On my forearms they appeared as quickly as I could wipe them off. You can only just feel them and I certainly wasn't bitten, but they were a nuisance all the same, and I wondered what ecological imbalance had given rise to their proliferation. Surely, I thought, they would be to the taste of ladybirds, for example, but I didn't see any. I could think of several reasons why they might have been attracted to me, none of which I could do much about – the shiny forehead, the giant, bright red rucksack, all those pheromones, not to mention the fried haggis on my breath – but corn lice are strange things. It is a fact that they are drawn to pictures in houses. They can find their way under the glazing and I have seen any number so entombed inside the smallest of prints. By slapping my head, neck, arms and thighs, I must have smudged thousands. From a distance my walking shorts could have been mistaken for lederhosen – I must have looked odd – and to pass as a festival dancer in Bavaria all I would have needed was a different hat and a mug of foaming beer! I obtained the beer, along with a bowl of soup (not rabbit) at The Glenfarg Inn and then followed the fast-flowing River Farg for about four miles down the glen. Ready for another stop, I was disappointed to find The Bein Inn, a beautiful, 15th-century drovers' inn, closed for the afternoon.

    The land was lower and flatter at that point, in marked contrast, I felt sure, to the terrain further north. The road took me to Bridge of Earn (the river flows into the Firth of Tay, a few miles to the east) and then, parallel to the M90, up to a saddle, where there is a busy interchange, Perthshire's answer to Spaghetti Junction.[43] While I walked, dark clouds had gathered, the air became still and close and, in the time it took me to retrieve my waterproofs, a terrible thunderstorm broke. I made for the shelter of a concrete flyover and cowered for a few minutes, thinking 'this will do'. The gods' fury proved short-lived but, once the thunderclaps had subsided to an occasional rumble, we were left with rain. This I found preferable to the echo of the traffic under the viaduct, the stale exhaust, and the knobbly paving on which I was uncomfortably perched.

Soon enough and through the wet, I could make out the River Tay. Nestling on its shores, I could also see what is often referred to as the "Fair City" and sometimes referred to as the "Gateway to the Highlands".

Perth is a fine city by any standards. Although tour guides probably exaggerate when it is claimed that the city was once Scotland's capital, it is an important centre …and certainly was around the time of the unfortunate King James I (of Scotland) – the same fellow who had blazed the trail for me, over the bridge at Cramond. He held court in Perth and, if ever there was a monarch who literally sealed his fate, then this was he. Apparently, with many enemies and hounded by assassins, his end came one night in February 1437. So the story goes, when hammering was heard at the door, he prised up a floorboard and hid in a sewer pipe. King James might well have escaped into the courtyard below. Unfortunately, by his own orders, the opening of the pipe had recently been sealed off, for the reason that tennis balls had been lost in the duct. What agony the realisation must have been as the cowering and trapped monarch awaited the coup de grâce, and what little consolation it would have been to find the missing balls!

---

[43] Spaghetti Junction is the nickname of the complex 18-route interchange with the M6 motorway in the Gravelly Hill area of Birmingham.

CHAPTER 14: LOCH LEVEN – PITLOCHRY

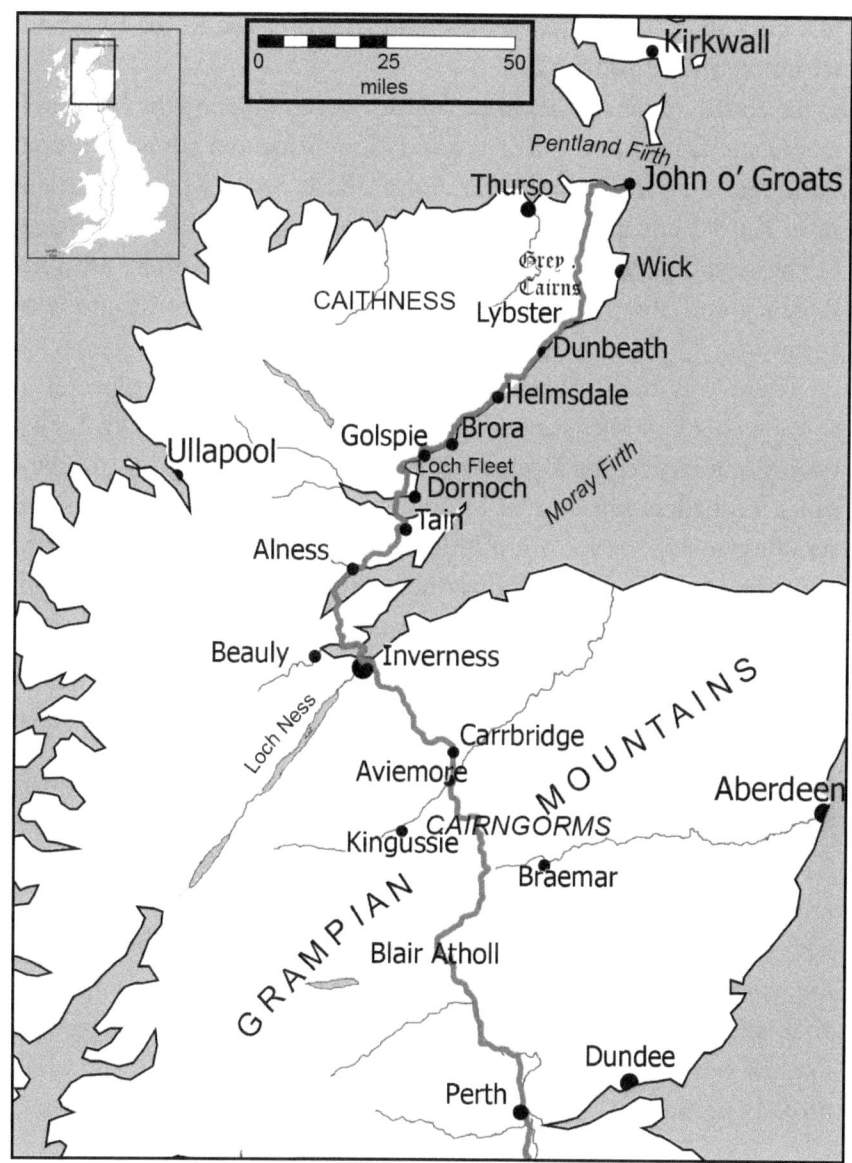

March to the Far North.

Just after that, his injured widow, and their son (James II) fled, and set up court in Edinburgh.

Perth still retains an air of prosperity and grandeur, which it takes from its setting on the wide river and its architecture. Some medieval buildings survive, including St. John's Kirk, from where a certain John Knox[44] once had a few choice words to say on a sensitive issue of the day! The Old Academy dates from 1771 and there are fine Regency and Victorian buildings, as well as some worthy modern additions.

There was more lightning, naturally of the forked type, as I scampered across the elegant, open parkland known as 'South Inch', towards the city centre. Dodging puddles and thinking of those under-nines footballers who had, at that time, recently been in the news for standing together in a big puddle during the thunderstorm which had stopped their game, directly beneath one of the dads' large and steel-shafted golfing umbrella (about twenty ended up in Maidstone Hospital with various degrees of electrical burns – mercifully none fatal) I said to myself:

"At least I'll go out with a bang!"

Via the tourist information centre, I made my way to Perth's youth hostel and there booked for myself what turned out to be the very last bed. For this, I breathed a big sigh of relief, as the idea of more walking did not appeal. By the microwave I met an Australian girl whose adventure put mine into perspective – she was travelling around the world, alone, cycling. It sounded an impossible journey and with an image of her muffled in furs peddling over the ice caps, I suggested that she was probably just coming up to halfway around. Of course, it turned out that hers was more a world tour than a circumnavigation *à*

---

[44] John Knox (1513-72) was a Scottish minister, theologian and writer. He was the leader of the country's Reformation and the founder of the Scottish Presbyterian Church.

CHAPTER 14: LOCH LEVEN – PITLOCHRY

la Phileas Fogg[45], but it emphasised that not everyone was as obsessive as I was about covering every inch.

In fact, the majority of hostellers that night were cyclists. Back in the male dormitory, they were swapping stories of pedal power and punctures. It didn't take me long to get to sleep and I slept soundly, for cyclists are healthy types with good lungs and clear heads. Fresh air is good for you, as we were told at school, and there were no loud snorers, I think; if there were, I was too tired to be disturbed, or perhaps, with my own Zs, I was drowning them out anyway!

The morning was crisp and bright, the rain-washed pavements were clean and dry, and the River Tay sparkled dazzlingly in the sunshine. I walked back into town to buy a large-scale map of Northern Scotland, which made me feel good, and then along the riverbank, where I was mildly surprised to find cricket grounds, for, unlike football, golf, fishing, hunting, curling, tossing the caber, or even rugby, cricket is not a sport one immediately associates with Scotland.

The first pitch looked especially good. There were brilliant white sight screens and green, green grass cut in beautiful stripes. I tried to remember why it is that vegetation does 'green up' after thunder and lightning. It is something to do with nitrogen fixation, as well as the watering, but whatever the reason, that morning the North Inch parklands were certainly verdant.

I marched past Balhousie Castle, which houses The Black Watch regimental museum and, continuing to follow the river, looked across towards Scone Palace (where every one of the forty-two crowned kings of Scotland took oath) before I came to the town of Luncarty.

A car had broken down by the side of the road. I approached and found the driver in floods of tears. I am not very good at these sorts of things, but my arrival seemed to distract her to a degree, and I asked

---

[45] Phileas Fogg is the protagonist in Jules Verne's 1873 novel who sets out to go *Around the World in Eighty Days*.

if I could help. Her engine had overheated; not only that, but she had scalded her hand and arm with boiling radiator water. She had already phoned a garage and as it turned out, she didn't have long to wait because a tow truck came along within minutes, by which time she had rallied a good deal. I left them to it, but then, coming to the main road, I realised why that unfortunate motorist had run into trouble: due to resurfacing, there was a massive traffic jam.

The northbound A9 resembled the clockwise M25 on a foggy Monday morning, apart from this was Scotland and a beautiful, hot and sunny day. I stepped in between the stationary cars and surveyed the line of overheated drivers, right arms dangling out of wound-down windows or fingers drumming hot tin roofs – or are they steel? The inside lane had been coned off for as far as the eye could see and, frustratingly from the motorists' point of view, there was absolutely no sign of workmen, tarmac lorries or resurfacing plant! I hadn't planned to use the A9 just there, but it seemed too good an opportunity to pass by, for while the lane may have been closed to vehicular traffic, there was nothing to stop me from using it. And so I added to the frustration of those stuck in the jam by strolling past a good deal quicker than they were going. To hot children hanging out of the back of heavily laden holiday cars, I smiled, waved or pulled faces as seemed appropriate and exchanged banter with people who called out things.

Several other cars had overheated and limped into my lane. There wasn't much I could do or say but I remembered a van I used to have which had to be driven with the heater on full blast, which gave me a few more miles before 'the kettle boiled', because its radiator had as many little perforations as a Tetley tea bag.

I could smell the new tarmac before I saw it, but, after at least two miles, I came to where the work was in progress. The air shimmered in the terrific heat above the machinery as bare-torsoed workmen shovelled and raked and rolled. They were moving slowly southwards,

CHAPTER 14: LOCH LEVEN – PITLOCHRY

but behind them the newly surfaced lane was also coned off. I had no wish to spoil it with bootprints and so walked right next to the traffic, which was starting to move. Cars which earlier I had passed, now passed me, and there was more banter and tooting. The new surface was firm enough to take my weight, which was just as well, because the line of traffic was by this time thundering by at high speed, each driver no doubt keen to make up lost time and glad to have moving air circulating once more. Soon enough, the cones angled off and with both lanes of the dual carriageway open, and no footway, I took the first track leading away from the main road that I came to, and headed into the country.

Finding myself in the midst of what, on first impression, seemed to be vineyards (on closer inspection these turned out to be fields of loganberries), I was tempted to indulge in a spot of 'scrumping', but was put off the idea by the sound of fierce barking which came from the nearby farmhouse. I looked down at my left wrist; the tooth mark had long faded beneath suntan, or dirt, or corn lice DNA, but the scratch on my watch was as clear as the memory of my encounter with 'the hound of the Staffordshire and Worcester Canal', and I decided to stay my side of the fence!

Near the hamlet of Tullybelton, I stopped on a minor road at an attractive bridge over a burn. On the wall, I sat and watched trout swimming beneath me in the clear water. I sprinkled my last crumbs of bread and cheese to see if there were any takers, but my offerings were ignored. Ahead of me, the heather-clad hills leading to Strathbraan looked inviting but I was unsure of the mountain route to Aberfeldy, as I did not have a detailed map. Furthermore, I was low on provisions, and opted instead to continue on the quiet lane into the town of Bankfoot.

One of the least successful bright ideas I had during those weeks was to store drink bottles jammed inside the roll of my foam camping mattress, which itself was secured by special straps to the back of my rucksack, somewhere behind my bottom. This was simply so that I could get at the drink 'on the march' without having to stop and remove the whole load. As I have explained before, maintaining a walking rhythm was important to me. All that had to be done was reach behind, slurp and return. The problem was that protruding bottles increased my width. That day I had completely forgotten that one such glass Lucozade bottle was there, and my entrance through the narrow doorway into the first pub in Bankfoot was spectacular. The bottle crashed to the tiled floor with the inevitable consequence. My blushing order at the bar was unusual:

"A pint of cider... and a dustpan please, barman!"

By mid-afternoon it was extremely hot. My feet were so sore that several times I had to sit down by the road and, wincing, rubbed away at the puffy, pink skin on the bottom of my feet or raised them alternately, because that seemed to help.

On a far smaller scale than the roadworks I'd seen that morning, a couple of Geordie navvies were moving along that road, filling potholes. They passed me twice in their yellow truck and the second time I caught up with them, one turned to me, leant on his tamper and without a smile delivered a stark message:

"You aren't going to make it." It wasn't a question, it was a statement of fact and it hit me hard. Nor did I quite know how to respond. Perhaps he was right. My progress that day had been slow and was getting slower but, having come that far, it just wasn't the way I had been thinking. In the end, I smiled bravely and gave what (rather unconvincingly) came out as a glib retort borrowed from the playground when, for example, a child is told that they are not going to be invited to go to so-and-so's birthday party:

..."Oh yes, I am."

As I walked on, with back straighter than normal and trying very hard not to limp, I practised the same phrase under my breath, aiming for a more assertive tone. Nodding like an Olympic high jumper

CHAPTER 14: LOCH LEVEN – PITLOCHRY

at the start of his run-up, psyching himself up for an attempt at a personal best, I continued to recite: "Oh yes, I am. Oh yes, I am! I am going to make it ... amn't I?"

The tonic that my doubting and drooping spirit needed came only a few painful miles down the road, when I came once more to the River Tay at Dunkeld. Just downstream from Telford's fine town bridge, I was sitting, barefoot, on the bank and looking across the wide and brilliantly blue, sparkling waters when, right on cue, an osprey swooped down to the water, midstream.

With the appearance of a small eagle, and wingspan of just over a metre, ospreys were hunted to the verge of extinction in Britain by fishermen fearful for their trout and salmon. Indeed, there were no breeding pairs at all for a period of around forty years prior to the 1950s when bird experts encouraged ospreys from Scandinavia to breed in Inverness-shire. Since then, numbers have risen, but even so, they are a great rarity and I felt privileged to have seen one at all.

There is a ruined cathedral in Dunkeld, which dates back to the 9th century and into which coach parties of hot Americans were crowding. The information centre nearby was also crowded, with narrow aisles between racks of postcards and leaflets. Recalling my accident earlier in the day, and sensing a possible repeat, I manoeuvred gingerly past the souvenir mugs and ashtrays without making a purchase. I headed for the peace and quiet of Dunkeld's centenary garden, which was specially constructed to commemorate no lesser personage than the inimitable Peter Rabbit.[46]

It seems that Beatrix Potter holidayed in Dunkeld as a child. Nowadays, the young, or the young at heart, can explore these grounds looking for statues of all their favourite characters. For my part, I ate a packet of digestives on a grassy bank in the shade of a

---

[46] Beatrix Potter's children's classic *The Tale of Peter Rabbit* has been translated into 36 languages, including ancient Egyptian hieroglyphs. It has sold more than 45 million copies.

young Scotch pine alongside 'Big P' himself. I offered him a biscuit but he didn't respond – presumably he was too full of lettuces, French beans and radishes.

Making a mental note to return to the garden with my own children, if ever I got to our John o' Groats rendezvous, I loaded up and recrossed the bridge, one eye on the river, in hope of a further osprey sighting, and the other on the line of cars and coaches passing at a range of at least three inches.

Leaving the tourists and townsfolk behind, I found a minor road which twisted through trees into the river valley high above the main A9, along which I could hear the traffic racing below. At one point there was an almighty crash. I could not see what had happened, for the planting was dense, nor was there any way down. The sickening smash jerked me back to something which happened when I was a student. A young racer lost control of his car on a long bend, on the edge of the campus, and it somersaulted along the pavement towards me: Then, I had jumped into the bushes and not knowing what to expect, was amazed to see the driver and his passenger emerge, without a scratch, which was certainly more than could be said for the car! Here, in Perthshire, I fully expected to hear sirens of ambulance and police, but none came, at least while I was within earshot. All I could do was to hope that everyone was all right.

When, eventually, my road dropped down through the trees to rejoin the expressway, the sun was much lower and was casting golden-yellow streaks in beams through thin cloud. It appeared very much as a child draws the sun, a yellow disc with lines coming out of it. The phenomenon was short-lived and, to my considerable disappointment, my efforts to photograph it met with only limited success.

It was dusk by the time I came to a road sign which read: 'Pitlochry 5' – and dark by the time I got there. Those few miles were among the most gritty and painful of the entire journey. For most of the time I

CHAPTER 14: LOCH LEVEN – PITLOCHRY

could see the street lamps and the Victorian resort's elaborate skyline. As the road was direct, it was just a question of left, right, for as long as it took, which was about two hours.

My mind was numb from blocking the pain in my feet, to the extent that when, eventually, I checked the map, I misinterpreted it. Icons showed that town has information, a museum, other tourist features and camping. I walked to the place on the map where the camping sign was, a little out of town, before realising that the map-makers had just lined up the symbols underneath the word 'Pitlochry'. All the features, of course, were in the town and it was only for reasons of clarity that their icons were spaced out, as I should have known. At John o' Groats, at the other end of the same map, for example, and by the same token, there is also information, a museum and camping, all of which are in the sea! It was an agonising mistake at that time and very nearly the straw which broke the backpacker, for I was utterly shattered by the time I found the site. It was as much as I could do to pitch tent and hobble to the shower block. Twenty pence bought a few minutes of warm water after which sleep was the only possibility.

CHAPTER 15

Pitlochry – Carrbridge

IN WHICH
...o'er crag and torrent, my Cairngorm crossing takes me into the "Pass of Foreboding" and I hear the clatter of cloven hooves.

I had breakfast by the River Garry, watching a fisherman who was standing midstream in waders. I was not certain, but I believed I had seen him in similar pose the evening before. It could have been someone else, but I preferred to imagine that he had stood there all night, dedicated, hungry, going for a record, or just plain unlucky. Investigating the town, I came across dozens of knitwear shops and hundreds of hotels, coach parks and the Bell's whisky visitor centre.

The river has been dammed, by Loch Faskally, around which the people of Pitlochry can enjoy attractive woodland walks. I took one trail along the east bank. The path had been constructed by the electricity company responsible for the dam. It snaked back and forth between the trees and the shore. In dappled light, and on soft ground to suit my tender tootsies, it made for pleasant and relaxed walking, although my overall progress was slow. I emerged at the foot of the Pass of Killiecrankie, where I filled up with wild raspberries growing on a rough bank beside the path. They tasted especially soft and sweet (there may have been some rain during the night) and they were plentiful enough for me to pick and consume several handfuls in no time. I remembered how, in Cornwall and in Cumbria, the berries had rescued me. Here, with the mighty Cairngorm Mountains before me, I ate for pleasure rather than out of necessity.

The pass itself is dramatic. There is a deep gorge through which

CHAPTER 15: PITLOCHRY – CARRBRIDGE

not only the river, but also a railway and three roads squeeze. In 1689, Jacobite rebels under Bonnie Dundee knocked six bells out of English government troops in a famous battle there. The visitor centre at Killiecrankie gives the full story. I crabbed around it for a few minutes but, keen to press on, made an exit on the arrival of a coach party. These days, the main strategic route out of the pass would be the A9, which is impressively engineered with long viaducts at that point. Troops could make a hasty exit along it, although guerrilla tactics in that terrain would be as effective today as they had been in the 17th century.

I followed the old road to the place known as Bridge of Tilt and from there, onwards into Blair Atholl. In the well-stocked village stores I bought food to last me about three days, including enough biscuits and chocolate to supply an illicit midnight feast in the second-form dormitory. Contemplating the scale and the grandeur of the scenery, I munched my way through a mountain of bread and cheese in parkland to the south of Blair Castle. Although my journey had taken me over high ground including Bodmin Moor and Dartmoor, the Mendips, the Cotswolds – and, of course, the whole Pennine Chain, before tackling the Southern Uplands, I knew that none of this was remotely comparable to the route ahead. I didn't need a map to tell me that this was geography in a different league. I also knew that even in high summer, the mountains would need to be treated with respect. The words of my guidebook resonated in my head: 'Do not think that just because you have walked all the way from Cornwall you are tougher than the elements'.[47] High up in the hills, conditions can change rapidly and although, with my full pack, I was already better equipped than often I have been when climbing or walking

---

[47] *Land's End to John o'Groats: A choice of footpaths for walking the length of Britain*, by Andrew McCloy (Coronet Books, 1994). This book is absolutely superb. It's really well written and provides a tremendous amount of useful information for anyone contemplating anything of this sort.

in Snowdonia, I nevertheless made some additional purchases: mint cake, renowned for its energy-boosting high calorific value; spare batteries for my torch; and whisky for medicinal consumption during blizzards and other situations.

With clear blue skies, a light breeze and plenty of warm sunshine, and with birdsong and bumblebees at the clover, it didn't seem very wintry. In fact, conditions were ideal for dozing in the grass. I stretched out but there was a knot in my stomach – induced, I felt sure, by a sense of anticipation as much as from the cheese overdose, and my eyelids didn't seem to want to shut, so I reorganised my rucksack, rechecked the map and began my mountainous adventure.

I had chosen to make my way up Glen Tilt, which meant returning first to Bridge of Tilt and then following a woodland path through a beech hanger beside the river.

To my left was the castle, bright and impressive, home to the Duke

Beech hanger near Blair Atholl.

of Atholl and his private army. Blair Castle's castellation is Victorian, but the tower within is 13th century and it has survived various sieges and attacks through history, including the explosive impact made by Cromwell's forces in 1652.

Just then, I came face to face with a red squirrel who had scampered onto the path from between the trees. I froze and so did he, apart from the twitching nose. Very slowly I reached behind me and, groping in a side pocket of the rucksack, pulled out my Minolta. Still the squirrel waited, until the moment I lifted the camera to my face, when he made his move. Quick as a flash, indeed quicker than mine, he ran around the back of the nearest tree and shot up out of sight. I couldn't really blame him: in those parts men with guns are common and, after all, did not trophy hunters compound the plight of his ancestors, decimated, as it was, by epidemic disease? "Better safe than sorry" had obviously served him well, for he was most certainly bright-eyed and bushy-tailed!

There are a number of dwellings on the path up Glen Tilt, the sort of places to which home delivery pizza services would carry a surcharge, even though the track is driveable for a long way. I remembered working years ago in a job which required me to deal with vehicle contract hirers and to negotiate the minutiae of what constituted "fair wear and tear": cars hired to people who live by the sea rust quickly in the salty air, for example, but I wondered how those companies would react if a car were returned after three years of bumping up Glen Tilt with its suspension shot. The lumps and bumps were also taking their toll on my feet. I trod gingerly over the stones, if I had to, but wherever possible walked on springy grass beside the track. I did not yet realise it, but my thinning boots were reaching a critical minimum just at the time when I would need them to give me the most protection.

Apart from a hardy family on rented mountain bikes, whom I met by one of the bridges, I saw no one at all until early evening when a large figure approached, dishevelled and perspiring. He was looking for somewhere to camp and asked me:

"Is there a bothy near here?" His voice was hoarse, as if his throat was dry and he spoke with an accent which I found hard to place, possibly Danish.

"I don't think so." I knew my map wasn't detailed enough to help and I hadn't seen any such shelter on the way up. "But there are plenty of good places to pitch tent on grass by the river." Of that I was certain, because I had been keeping an eye out for such places for myself, although I intended to get higher still. He didn't seem convinced, so I ventured further advice.

"Or there's the campsite at Blair Atholl."

"How far is that?"

I paused, looked at my watch and thought. He looked very tired, but it would be literally downhill all the way and there was enough light.

"About three hours."

"Three hours!" he repeated in astonishment. I supposed he would have preferred to hear something like 'Oh, just around that corner beyond those rocks', but unfortunately for him, it simply wasn't like that, high up in the heart of the Grampians.

As he headed off down the path I called out after him, "Good luck!" Wherever he ended up he would be sure to wake up with aching limbs and sore feet – something I knew a thing or two about!

The majesty of the scenery quite distracted me from any thoughts of self-pity. I continued to tread delicately as a matter of instinct whilst surveying the panorama. Behind me, the views extended down the glen over the plantations and across the Highlands for mile upon mile into the dim distance; ahead of me and to the sides, the valley rose, steeper and deeper, heather-clad.

I was marvelling and eating when I saw the first herd of red deer on the other side of the valley. They are commonplace in that region,

CHAPTER 15: PITLOCHRY – CARRBRIDGE

Looking back south, down Glen Tilt.

The suspension bridge at Falls of Tarf, Glen Tilt, which was built after a boy drowned there in August, 1879.

a fact which visitors will be aware of, if only from the large, public notices about the deer posted along the route, for example at Forest Lodge. In plain terms (and in some detail) are set out the reasons why deer are culled. Now I may have been well wide of the mark, but it struck me from the existence *and the ton*e of these notices that among the visitors must be those opposed to the cull.

"Don't be so silly and sentimental," the notices seemed to say, "learn the facts about management of the Highland economy"; and also, "You'd better keep your heads down!"

For my part, I kept a sharp lookout and, sure enough, before long, I sighted the animals but I had the distinct impression that the deer had spotted me before I had seen them. In fact, they have an incredible sense of smell and, although their field of stereoscopic vision is small, each eye sees a wide angle and, of course, there are many eyes on the lookout in a herd. A large stag a little away from the main group was watching me intently, I could tell, but the remainder continued to graze. I stopped where I was and surreptitiously reached for a snack. The path leading up the glen took me to within about a hundred metres of the deer but, in the few minutes that passed while I finished my cheese roll and got to that point, they had moved, not far, but enough to maintain a safe distance.

There were more of the animals, including one much larger herd, along the way in the last few miles of that day, enough that when I pitched tent on high ground beside the infant River Dee, I wondered if I would have hoofed visitors during the night. Thoughts of death by trampling kept me awake for at least three minutes, after which the soothing babble of running water and gentle drumming of some light rain on the tent roof carried me swiftly into unconsciousness.

The morning was damp and foggy, quite chilly. Packing up my equipment, I shivered, like Charles I might have done, but since I wore a thermal vest under my fleece my shiver probably related to the fact that ahead of me loomed three of the four highest mountains

CHAPTER 15: PITLOCHRY – CARRBRIDGE

in the UK. I contemplated making an ascent of Ben Macdui, but didn't scale it, even though I spotted what seemed to be the foot of an established way up or down. For one thing there was the weather – being lost in the fog on a mountain that I did not know, and which claims lives almost every year, hardly appealed – and neither was I properly equipped for climbing: if anything, I had too much on my back. What chance had I of shinning up a rock chimney, if I couldn't even get through a pub doorway? And there was another reason why I decided not to stray from the path. It was a question of time, because my family were even then in transit, heading north for a holiday in Inverness-shire. If I could cross the Cairngorms that day, we had worked out that our paths might cross, so onwards and upwards I went.

At one time, cattle were driven across the mountains between Deeside and Speyside; these days I suppose that hill walkers, climbers, eagle spotters and geologists use the Lairig Ghru rather more. Identifiable by the equipment they bore, I was to come across people in pursuit of each of these activities, with the exception of cattle droving, but not for some hours. At the time, it did not cross my mind that unless, like me, they had camped high up or set off in the small hours, anyone coming from Aviemore or Braemar simply couldn't have reached where I was. It all did seem a bit spooky. There may well have been people out there in the fog but I didn't see them and when I stopped to listen, I heard nothing at all except my own breathing and heartbeat. In that frame of mind, it wasn't long before I was imagining the clatter of so many stumbling hooves, mingling with moos of protestation and the cries of ghostly drovers lost in time. The image, I suppose was something like 'Rawhide meets Brigadoon'.[48]

I did my own share of stumbling, particularly on the other side

---

[48] *Rawhide* was a TV western series popular in the 1960s. Starring Eric Fleming and Clint Eastwood, the show told stories from a droving cattle drive, set in the 1860s.

of Lairig Ghru's 835-metre summit. The name loses something in translation from the Gaelic – it means 'Gloomy Pass' or 'Pass of Foreboding', although on that day the cloud lifted well before I had navigated its length, and there were stunning views of the mountains.

The upper part of the pass acts as a giant wind funnel and, once over the crest, I walked directly into a fierce northerly, which was strong enough to overbalance me time after time as I stepped from rock to rock. So worn down were the soles of my boots by then that bedroom slippers would have given me about as much protection. Balancing on pointed rocks was excruciating. I remember having to talk to myself along that stretch, and the few words with people coming up, such as "Hello, bit brighter now!" through gritted teeth, were not so much a comment on the weather and more a message of encouragement to my drooping spirits!

The path becomes less rocky further down and by the time I reached the tree line, where pine trees provided dappled shade and soft, spongy beds of fallen needles to step on, I felt strong enough when someone said, "Lovely day," to affirm, "Glorious!"

Aviemore was positively heaving with holidaymakers. The bars and burger bars were doing brisk trade. Youths in shell suits and back-to-front baseball caps walked up and down, or sat on benches drinking Coke. There were lots of large men in shorts and T-shirts, coachloads of camera-slung visitors from America, shoppers, cyclists, sailboarders, all manner of people, and all of them in sunglasses. I slipped through the throng with no desire to battle for overpriced designer lager in one of these neon-lit joints and, since I had no room in the pack for a souvenir Santa Claus in tartan, I put the bustle behind me without delay.

Once more surrounded by wide views and green space, and with four or five miles between myself and everyone in Aviemore, I was pacing along a minor road towards Carrbridge. A passing car tooted me. It was my wife and family.

CHAPTER 15: PITLOCHRY – CARRBRIDGE

People have asked how such a meeting could happen at all. I carried no mobile phone. In fact the last time we had spoken, I was on the other side of Britain's biggest mountain range, but the girls knew I was heading north and also that I would choose a minor road in preference to the roaring expressway. Taking the philosophical view that if I had fallen off a mountain or been eaten by an eagle there was little she could do about it anyway, my wife just drove along the road and let her own eagle eyes do the rest. We embraced, noted the precise location and then drove to Beauly.

CHAPTER 16

Carrbridge – The Morangie Forest

IN WHICH
...I explore the 'Capital of The Highlands' and plunge into the unknown.

Well rested, clean and with lovely fresh socks, at exactly the place I had reached the previous evening, I resumed the challenge around lunchtime. I wore spongy trainers: a boot inspection the previous evening had revealed grave deficiency and in spite of the bruising on my feet, there was a spring in my step. Furthermore, for the first time since Tewkesbury, I had no load to carry.

As I jogged into Carrbridge it started to rain. Had I got my waterproof? There were certainly 'pros' and 'cons' of travelling light! I didn't fancy a soaking at that moment and so took the familiar evasive action and darted into The Cairn Hotel, which is attractively situated by the town's historic bridge over the Duthil Burn. In the bar, I learned a little about the area. The burn, which flows fast and foamy at that point, collects cool, clear water from the Monadhliath Mountains to the east to feed the Spey near Grantown a few miles to the west.

The bridge itself, built in 1719, spans the river in a single, satisfying arch. Original mortar has been replaced with concrete but the stonework appears as it always must have done. Later on, I took a closer look and was surprised to see what I was sure would have been a sign prohibiting people from climbing on the historic bridge. But the sign gave a different message, which was polite and cautionary. Visitors were warned that the stones can sometimes be slippery and that the current beneath is strong. Presumably anyone who falls in

CHAPTER 16: CARRBRIDGE – THE MORANGIE FOREST

Carrbridge.

The "Black" Isle?

has the added ignominy of knowing, on the way down, that he had the chance to follow sensible advice… and chose to ignore it! In a macabre fashion, I wondered how many people and animals had taken the fatal plunge over the centuries. There again, if cattle and drovers could cope with the rocky old Lairig Ghru, then maybe a good number got over Carrbridge in one piece. In spite of the caution and the wet, I found the temptation to scramble over too strong … but didn't fall!

Out of Carrbridge, the road snakes up through forest planting and emerges back at the A9. I found an alternative route along stretches of an old military road constructed by General Wade in the road-building programme his soldiers executed in the 18th century. Off the main road I could enjoy the scenery rather better and spotted another herd of red deer grazing in rough ground near the forest, but also near to the road. It puzzled me that the animals seemed unperturbed by such things as HGVs and BMWs, but wouldn't trust me any closer than half a valley.

Even express haulage trucks slow down at Slochd Summit, but my legs carried me over the ridge without really changing gear. Since the cloud was down, I couldn't see very far. Conscious also that, with a later start than usual and a lengthy break for rain in Carrbridge, my progress had not been great, I decided to speed up. Earlier, almost by way of celebrating not carrying the pack, I had been jogging. Now, aided by the slope and with the wind behind me, I ran – quite fast. Feeling fit and without complaint from the body, I continued running for five or six miles, through the settlements at Findhorn Bridge and Tomatin, a centre for whisky distilling. I ran back out, onto and across the A9 to a point by Loch Moy and there I was once more intercepted by my family and rescued from more rain.

Imagine the shape of Scotland on a map and trace your finger clockwise around its outline and you will soon come to Inverness. It is to the Great Glen and the Moray Firth what Edinburgh is to

CHAPTER 16: CARRBRIDGE – THE MORANGIE FOREST

the Firth of Forth. Any Norse-fearing Highland chief worth his salt would have recognised its strategic value, and archaeological evidence points to the existence of settlements in the region dating back to the Stone Age. These days it is the commercial capital of the Highlands, servicing Scotland's north with bright lights, department stores, professional football, and so on. It is a cultural centre with museums, gardens and concert halls, and a focus on tourism. For me also, Inverness was a focal point. It was the last major centre of population through which I would pass, and the city had been a big target whenever I compartmentalised planning. As far as Inverness, I could draw on some form of recollection, places I had been to or through at some time. I had no such experience of anywhere further north than Inverness so, amongst any number of possible divisions, I tended to think of my walk in two bits: as far as Inverness, and beyond Inverness, into the unknown.

And so it was that very purposefully I strode out from my drop-off by Loch Moy, the final few miles into the city. Not wishing to be caught out again, the rucksack was back, although it contained little more than my waterproof clothing and a sandwich. Near the village of Daviot I was delighted that one of my speculative shortcuts took me away from the main road into a lovely, leafy dell and across the River Nairn via an elegant suspension footbridge, bouncy enough to bring out the child in anyone. The obvious temptations were recognised by polite notices at either end, encouraging bridge users to exercise restraint. Perhaps the odd baby had been jettisoned from its pram at some point, in much the same way that yelping toddlers in the playground can be sent skywards if see-sawing becomes too vigorous!

Passing signposts to Culloden[49] field, I followed my nose through contrasting areas of development, including that defining

---

[49] On the 16th April 1746 around 2,000 Jacobite soldiers were killed or mortally wounded in the decisive defeat inflicted by government forces at Culloden. The short and very bloody fight was the last pitched battle fought on British soil.

phenomenon of modern life, the retail park. I decided not to buy a new carpet for the living room and headed instead for the city centre where I found shade and some refreshment in an Irish bar, which looked rather less crowded than other similar establishments servicing the needs of thirsty shoppers, holidaymakers and office workers on lunch break.

There is an imaginative 'living history experience' at Inverness Castle. The costumed guides remain 'in character' from start to finish. In return for my admission money, having received "The King's Shilling" (the token payment for enlisting with the English Army in 1745), I was bullied by a worryingly realistic megalomaniac sergeant, taught how to use a musket, and told precisely what I could do with my shilling by the woman whose job it was to handle baggage. "Baggage" was the term used for women who, physically separated from their enlisted partners, seemed to have been used rather like carthorses, with the extra role of being with "brats" too young to fight. Furthermore, if any brat misbehaved, the nearest baggage would be beaten! What a life!

On the other bank of the Ness (which pedestrians can cross on suspension bridges) is St Andrew's Cathedral and, nearby, Balnain House, in which there is a museum of Highland music. I wanted to go there, and fulfilled something of an ambition when they let me play a set of bagpipes. I sat on the steps, working out fingerings and then played 'Scotland the Brave', after a fashion, with the bag wedged between my legs. This unorthodox method was the only way I could get enough pressure to make the chanter reed 'speak' and I realised just how much puff those pipers need. While I sat there, a group of Americans stepped over me. Perhaps it was a measure of how painful my playing must have been, but I didn't get a single tip!

I crossed town and, hoping to see seals and dolphins, I walked along the shore of the Beauly Firth for some way. The tide was out and, seeing rather a lot of mud and no aquatic mammals, I made for

CHAPTER 16: CARRBRIDGE – THE MORANGIE FOREST

the Kessock road bridge which carries the A9 over the Firth onto the Black Isle.

The bridge itself is certainly an impressive structure but it wasn't immediately apparent to me how to get onto it from my position by the water's edge without doubling back into town and following the road signs. In the end, I scrambled up the high banking, climbed over a fence, and only then spotted a pedestrian access up a flight of steps!

The view to the west, looking over the Beauly Firth, was quite something.

I was lining up a photograph when I became aware of someone approaching. It was a lad in his late-teens, bespectacled and basketball-booted, who came right up and stood beside me, leaning on the railings. He didn't say a word, perhaps so that the camera didn't shake, but it seemed a little odd. I said something like, "Pretty, isn't it?" For it was… but there was no reply. I put the camera away and walked on. Like an obedient dog 'on heel', my silent companion followed right behind. I didn't feel the least bit threatened, but I was nonetheless surprised that when I paused a second time, to view the scene looking back towards the city, he stopped again, too, only this time he spoke, very softly:

"Have you come far?"

It was not the first time I had been asked that, but now I was less well prepared with an answer. In fact, I could find no words as I considered his. He had been following right behind with my fluorescent notice staring him in the face for several minutes. I felt guilty for assuming my sign had been read and understood. After further pause for thought I replied.

"Well, I've been walking for about five weeks."

"Oh." The lad said nothing else until I added:

"… and I'm going to John o' Groats." Suddenly he became animated.

"John o' Groats!"

He clapped his hands together and rocked from foot to foot. "I've been there! There's a ferry..." He stopped, his expression fell, his eyes rolled backwards in his head and, like E.T. in the Spielberg movie[50], he outstretched a long finger mysteriously and said, "...But it's a long way!"

I knew, without looking, to what he was pointing, for I had seen it, from inside a car, a couple of times before. We had come to a green road sign. At the bottom, it read:

JOHN O' GROATS 120

Now, if you have ever been on a long motorway journey and, wishing the miles away, have used successive road signs to count down the distance to your destination, you will know how I felt about reaching that point.

John o' Groats, for its size, is extremely well signposted. I wondered whether there is any other hamlet signposted at such a distance. It seemed unlikely. Not counting the posers' fingerboard at Land's End, this sign is the furthest south that "Groats" appears. For me it triggered a final, if lengthy, countdown.

I was shown how to cross the road in safety and then escorted through a gap in the hedge to a path which led steeply up towards some houses. The lad went out of his way home to show me another path which took me back down to the level of the main road, but a little further on. Thanking him for his directions, I said that I was grateful for *any* route which took me away from the A9.

My temporary companion having returned home, I did soon find an alternative route along quiet lanes through farmland, where I strolled in afternoon sunshine by Highland cattle to one side, and experimental grain plantation on the other. The latter I took to be the work of research scientists involved in the whisky industry. Precise plots had been measured out for planting. By each one, a nameplate

---

[50] *E.T. the Extra-Terrestrial* (1982) Universal Pictures.

CHAPTER 16: CARRBRIDGE – THE MORANGIE FOREST

had been staked. 'Optic', I read, then 'Landlord'… and wondered how you do name a new strain of grain.

Near the village of Tore, I recognised our car coming down the lane towards me. My wife leant out of the window and told me that there was a good pub about a mile further on, and that she would have a pint of 'seventy shilling' waiting for me when I got there. You can imagine how my step quickened at that! The promised pint still had its frothy head when I arrived.

We returned to The Kilcoy Arms in the morning. The plan for that day was simply to press on 'up country' until I was collected again. There was no final rendezvous, with the understanding that I would opt for minor roads in preference to the expressway, that was unnecessary, and I set off again without all the camping paraphernalia weighing down my rucksack.

There was a cloudless, deep blue sky overhead, stretching to the horizon on every side. Scarcely living up to its name, the Black Isle glowed iridescent gold with fields of freshly cut wheat. Initially, I picked a path along the main road's dusty verges, which were scorched and also newly cut. Through heat haze above the tarmac I could see more deep blue, sapphire almost, shimmering and flashing with diamond white: it was the Cromarty Firth and I was heading for the road crossing north-east of Dingwall.

The bridge itself, in marked contrast to the crossing of Kessock, or for that matter at Queensferry, is low to the water. No tall ships would pass underneath for sure and, from a distance, it bears some resemblance to a railway embankment crossing low ground prone to flooding. Seal-spotting holidaymakers in camper vans evidently found it a pleasing spot to stop for a sandwich…and so it was, for a welcome cooling breeze was gently being funnelled up the Firth. Making the most of it, I walked slowly across, looking both ways, but especially out to sea.

Like millions of others, I would guess, I knew of Cromarty from the shipping forecast. The word is linked with others like Dogger, Fisher, Viking and North Finistère.[51] I would also guess, unless you have business on Rockall, or fish above Bailey's Bank that to many of us, these are words which carry little precise meaning.

I looked along the Firth to the sea beyond. At that moment, I classified myself along with anyone who had no interest in football but who could nevertheless tell you, with certainty, that the football club in Doncaster is Doncaster Rovers and not Doncaster Athletic, for example. I apologise if there does exist an outfit called Doncaster Athletic, but my point is that, even though I had never actually found myself in a stricken fishing vessel riding waves in a gale-force wind, I had at least seen 'sea area Cromarty'; even if I had never witnessed the Rovers in the passion of a thrilling cup tie with Rotherham or Scunthorpe United, I had at least been to the Belle Vue ground.[52] It was like that with many sights in the final part of my journey. After all, everything I came to was new to me, every place, every view, a new experience, and all the more vivid for being so.

On the other side of the bridge I found a way to get off the main road, taking a track over an unmanned railway crossing by the Foulis Estate. A straight and practically deserted lane took me into the village of Evanton. I found a bar at the Glen Glass Hotel, met a couple of very fit girls who were cycling the length of Britain (and who agreed with me that Cornwall is a very long county), and heard ghost stories from the locals. One such story concerned a 'white lady' and the Glen a little to the north-west. The tale was so compelling that I subsequently returned to the spot and drove up the glen out of curiosity. With broken and twisted trees, dark chasms and hidden

---

[51] The seas around the British Isles are divided into 31 named "sea areas", each associated with a geographical feature in the area's location. Seafarers listen to the BBC's longwave radio broadcasts for the "shipping forecast" and warnings of gales.

[52] From 1922 to 2006, the Belle Vue Stadium was the home of Doncaster Rovers F.C. The club now plays at Keepmoat Stadium.

CHAPTER 16: CARRBRIDGE – THE MORANGIE FOREST

features, Glen Glass is certainly an eerie place, an ideal haunt for spooks and, I should think, an excellent hunting ground for any would-be ghostbuster.

From Evanton, I walked a hot and sticky few miles into Alness, where the events which followed will stay with me forever! There is a road bridge and a separate pedestrian gangway which span a steep gorge, at the bottom of which flows the river Alness, narrow, dark, clear, cool and deep. It took me a moment to work out what was going on, for a number of people were gathered on the footpath on the bridge. Most were watching, but a handful of lads were daring each other to take the plunge. It looked a long way down, but I watched for several minutes and each boy who jumped re-emerged, seemingly undamaged. They first had to climb over steel girders and railings and having made the jump, there was a short swim to the riverbank and then a scramble up the steep bank, which was accomplished with the aid of exposed tree roots. I decided to climb down and enjoy the spectacle from below. I negotiated the descent and took some photographs of humans in flight.

"I think I touched the bottom this time!" a jumper exclaimed as he dripped past me on the stony shore. Like Brian Hanrahan, news reporter on the flight deck of the Invincible during the Falklands War, who famously "counted them all out and counted them all back",[53] I double-checked, from my new position, that everyone who disappeared into the water did actually reappear… And they continued to do so, to my continued surprise!

Back on top of the bridge, I interviewed some of the boys. One of them, named Sandy Wilson, who actually jumped from the top of the gantry, well above the height of the road (for extra thrill) told me that they weren't sure who had first thought of jumping, but that it was

---

[53] Hanrahan's words, which circumvented restrictions placed on reporting by the Ministry of Defence, allowed the British public to know that no British fighter planes had been shot down by Argentinian forces, as had been claimed.

great fun and you only ever hurt your feet... and that wasn't so bad if you wore trainers. The boys were as interested in me as I was in them. They looked at my rucksack and read my sign.

"Look at those muscles on his legs!" said one, before taking another plunge. The longer I stayed chatting and answering questions, the clearer it became that I had to jump. In hindsight, it was pure madness but, burning up under the sun and cajoled by the boys, I soon found myself standing on the wrong side of the railings, wearing only my walking shorts and my cricket shoes, clinging to the metalwork. I remembered talking to that man on the bridge outside Hawick and thought about the gypsy boys jumping there. How crazy *that* had seemed! Something inside me rang alarm bells and for a moment I fell back on a logical train of thought. I wondered since (as I tell my students):

"FORCE = MASS x ACCELERATION"

...and since *my* mass was undoubtedly much greater than any of the others, whether I would hit the bottom! So much for the logic: I took a couple of deep breaths and then, with my rucksack and my entire possessions, including money, camera and spectacles, all abandoned on the pavement, I stepped off.

I remember seeing the foliage of trees flash past. Sandy had pointed out the deepest part, over which I had positioned myself moments before. The exhilaration was acute, as I accelerated towards the water and when I hit it, all my bodily senses were instantaneously overloaded. For a second or two I could do nothing, but as my descent slowed, I kicked and pulled hard, bobbing back up to the surface. I could not tell if I had hit the bottom, or if I was injured. All I knew was that I was alive and that I had lived preceding moments with an intensity beyond compare.

The current was noticeable but not strong enough to wash me away so that, breathless from the shock, rather than the exertion of swimming, I reached the bank. I seemed to be intact and followed

CHAPTER 16: CARRBRIDGE – THE MORANGIE FOREST

Bridge jumping at Alness.

the dampened route once more back up to the bridge. I approached the boys with a triumphant grin. Sandy led some slightly less than spontaneous cheering, which stopped abruptly when someone asked:

"Are you going again?"

I explained that once was enough for me. Attempts to persuade me otherwise were short-lived, and the general view seemed to be expressed by one boy who was ready to forgive me for not staying to develop my bridge-jumping style, on the grounds of my advanced age and the fact that, as he put it:

"Our teacher would ne'er do that. No way!"

As I lifted the rucksack onto my back all the boys jumped, one after the other, peeling off, as do fighter aircraft in formation flying. They waved, rather than saluted, as they fell, but the effect was the same.

The afternoon was still very warm. My shorts had dried in no time and I felt only the occasional drip on my calf from the cricket shoes which dangled by their laces from the back of my pack. I passed through farmland, on the outskirts of Alness into the Morangie Forest and continued, with a few stops to pick and eat wild raspberries from beside the track, for another eight or nine miles, which were spent in quiet reflection.

The planting in this forest is neither as dense nor as oppressively close to the path as in the Kielder Forest. Instead of either full sunshine or black shadow, I could enjoy dappled shade, especially as late afternoon became early evening. The terrain was not difficult, the air was cooler, my pack was not heavy and I knew that I had a soft bed for the night. A strong sense of well-being had come over me, even before my wife pulled up. After all, had I not taken the plunge at Alness and lived to tell the tale? With John o' Groats only a few days away, nothing could stop me now, could it? Nothing or nobody.

CHAPTER 17

The Morangie Forest – Golspie

IN WHICH
...disaster strikes at Loch Fleet, and a radical rethink is called for.

David Amos, aged twelve and a family friend, was also staying in Beauly on the farm with his family, where mine was based. Whilst I had spent the days walking, David and everyone else had been doing what most people would do on holiday in those parts: visiting castles, having picnics, and so on. Probably bored with chasing his little sister and my girls around the paddock, David had set on the idea of joining me to walk and camp, for a time and distance to be determined by factors such as how far he could or wanted to go and whether or not, or for how long, we could put up with each other. Years earlier, as an excitable pageboy on my wedding day, David first tied the tails of my tailcoat and then all but ended forever my conjugal prospects by fetching me an unprovoked, crumpling and eye-watering blow to my nether regions which forced a postponement of marital consumation. As we all know (or will come to know), time is a great healer. That boy seemed to me to have mellowed, all was forgiven many times over, and I agreed to let him tag along. Accordingly, the next morning, two cars stopped at the point from which my wife had collected me the previous evening. Two rucksacks, one large and one smaller, were donned, and the two of us set out, side by side.

We came to the settlement of Lamington, where there is a school but, since there are hardly any houses, I imagined that there can't have been a great number of children on its roll. We continued at a brisk pace and soon dropped down into the historic town of Tain.

Granted its Charter in AD 1000, Tain is a royal burgh and a

handsome place, but David and I didn't bother to visit the old tollbooth or any of the historical buildings, including the famed St Duthac memorial Church, stopping only at, respectively, the confectioners and the bank. We crossed the railway at Tain's station, via a footbridge (David is a railway enthusiast) and made our way onto the seashore. So far, so good.

My intent was to 'beach-walk' along the sandy mouth of the Dornoch Firth, rejoining the A9 at the new road bridge. In the event, it seemed better to loop back into Tain and walk the pavements, because the sand was very soft and also because David couldn't resist jumping back and forth over the rocks of the sea defences, in a fashion that brought to mind Storm, the canine companion of famous walker Hamish Brown. They both walked from John o' Groats to Land's End, but whilst Hamish's route was long enough, some 3000 miles, he wrote that his dog must have covered many times that distance![54]

With David walking 'to heel' we passed the Glenmorangie distillery, visitor centre, tasting and sales areas. I explained to David why, in pronunciation, the emphasis in Morangie is on the first and not the second syllable. David was unmoved, asking only:

"When can we stop for lunch?"

Remembering my own advice to the raw-footed Cotswold Way walkers and since we had barely been five miles, I told the lad that it would be better to press on for a while, but when, moments later, it came on to drizzle as we approached the bridge, I relented.

Inside the Dornoch Bridge Inn, I ordered something black and fizzy for David and treated myself to something a lot more palatable, a shot of the local 'water of life', asking a somewhat dour bartender if it travelled well. He gave me the same look as once I had received from a barmaid on-board a cross-channel ferry, of whom I had enquired: "Have you ever been to France before?" Nobody seemed to mind

---

[54] 'Hamish's Groats End Walk' by Hamish Brown (Gollancz, 1981).

CHAPTER 17: THE MORANGIE FOREST – GOLSPIE

The Beauly Firth.

The Dornoch Firth.

when David unpacked his lunch and tucked in, even though food was being served.

Suitably fortified, we set out again around one. Crossing the bridge, we were eyeballed by a seal, swimming alongside. Since neither one of us was carrying a fresh fish to lob in his direction, we left the animal to fend for himself.

On the other side of the crossing, we had the choice of dropping down into Dornoch, which, in hindsight, would have saved a lot of trouble, or ploughing a straighter furrow to the north along the roadside. I suppose at the back of my mind was the niggle that we might not get as far as I wanted... what amounted to doubling back didn't seem for the best so, unwisely, I sold David the idea of road walking for a little longer.

We made a number of stops along that stretch and the distances between breaks were ever decreasing. The plain fact was that the boy was tired out, but it was less obvious what to do about it, as we had passed the point of no return so far as the campsites at Dornoch were concerned, and there was nowhere suitable to pitch a tent. On either side of the road it was steep and rocky.

With much encouragement from me and a good deal of bravery from David, by early evening we had reached a place where the road drops down to the shore level, skirting an inlet known as Loch Fleet, a name which will haunt me as long as I live.

We climbed a barbed-wire fence and beyond a strip of brambles and gorse, found a wide, flat, grassy area, just above the beach. While I put up the tent, David, curiously reinvigorated, collected wood to build a fire which, in time, we lit and cooked over.

It was a good fire: David had done well with the wood... "I should think that'll do now!" I called, as another large timber was being dragged from the beach.

As the light faded we sat, staring glassy-eyed into the flames, saying little. David kept the fire well stoked, transferring branches from

CHAPTER 17: THE MORANGIE FOREST – GOLSPIE

his stockpile into the growing blaze. Sparks leapt high into the air, boosted by an onshore breeze. Whatever the perils of seafarers in sea area Cromarty that evening, they were unlikely to run aground in Loch Fleet, I mused, for David's blaze must have been visible halfway to Scandinavia!

The fire's warmth, fresh air and exercise had made me rather dozy. Retiring to the tent some metres away, I felt sure that David wouldn't be far behind. I left the tent door open but zipped shut the fine, synthetic fabric mosquito mesh, calling through it:

"Kick sand over it when you've had enough."

Normally I slept on my back diagonally in the tent, to give myself more room, stowing my kit in the triangular spaces on either side. With another person to fit in, it was necessary to put some of the equipment outside the tent, but having done that, I snuggled down to one side. Before long, I was barely conscious and only faintly aware of the occasional 'snap', as David gathered more branches to fuel the fire.

I do not know at what time David came to bed, but I certainly felt him kneel on my foot when he did!

An hour or two must have passed before I was violently disturbed. David snapped upright and shrieked:

"What the..."

I was wide awake, too, but it took a moment to realise just what was happening. Later on, David related that, at first, he thought he had wet himself, and my own recollection in the very instant of waking, was that David had spilt a drink over me. The truth was that what must have been an exceptionally high tide had rushed in and was filling the tent. From nothing, we were ankle-deep in no time. David was first out. Having pulled on his trainers, he stepped straight into the sea and waded back towards the gorse bushes. Fumbling frantically in the pitch-dark, I gathered up anything to hand and relayed it to David, who was shivering at the water's edge. My intention was to

The Boy David.

save the tent, if possible, so I groped beneath the water for the pegs. Fortunately they all came out easily and I was able to grab the top of the dome and lift the whole structure. One of the diagonal cross members split under the weight of the water within but I managed to lift it clear. An important find was the torch, with which I located various objects such as floating boots. Some equipment, including cooking pots, eluded the search and was lost, but the majority of our kit was collected. Unfortunately, of course, everything was completely soaked.

Quick thinking was called for, as our situation was not great. This was more than a nuisance and in the shocking realisation that we had been only moments from drowning, I had to work out a plan of action. Barefoot, in the brambles and gorse, I struggled to pack everything away. All I could do was to put the dryer things at the top of my sack. I wrung out the sleeping bags and loaded mine, together with the tent, which was not easy to pack away in those conditions, towards the bottom. In my quick-drying walking shorts and thermal

CHAPTER 17: THE MORANGIE FOREST – GOLSPIE

vest, I was better off than poor David, whose denim jeans were saturated, heavy and cold.

As it turned out, we had little choice but to press on up the road, towards the small town of Golspie, which lies about four miles to the north of Loch Fleet. It is the administrative centre for Sutherland and, importantly for us, has a railway station. Trains come from Thurso and Wick in the very far north and make stops, mainly on the north-east coast, and head for Inverness (although it is still possible to go all the way cross-country, through Strath Bran on a picturesque ride which terminates at Kyle of Lochalsh, by the controversial bridge over the sea to Skye). If we could get to Golspie, I could put David on a train south.

We plodded slowly along, in near darkness, with David a couple of paces ahead of me. We used the torch only when traffic approached. There were no cars, to my recollection, just the occasional heavy goods vehicle, loud and scary, with full beamers ablaze. I taught David the trick of closing or covering one eye in the bright light to preserve night vision, but before too long this became unnecessary. We were the best part of seven hundred miles north of London and dawn breaks early in the summer months. Although it was grey, rather than coloured light, which fell on the road in front of us, one had the feeling that the sun wasn't too far below the horizon and, by the time we reached the outskirts of the town, it seemed more like day than night.

At the station the priority was to find a timetable. I was sure there would be a long, long wait, perhaps the trains only ran on alternate days, but it wasn't anything like that.

"What day is it?" I asked benumbed David.

"Dunno ...umm. Thursday."

There was a good commuter service starting early in the morning. Even so, we had a couple of hours to kill. David flopped onto a bench on the platform and closed his eyes. Beside him, with my fleece zipped up over my chin for comfort and warmth, I sat and stared, collecting my thoughts. It was still too early to telephone but, if I timed it right, I could get a message to David's parents via the farmhouse, to meet him off the train at Muir of Ord, which is not far from where they were staying. If that failed, or even if the exhausted lad overslept and ended up in Inverness (which was a possibility) he himself could phone or get a taxi. Waking up on the west coast at Kyle of Lochalsh may have presented a few problems, however, so I double-checked the timetables to make sure I put him on the right train! Again, I had no cause for concern.

For my own part there were decisions to make. Having come this far, there was no way that a minor setback such as a near drowning, or losing all one's kit would stop me going onwards and upwards. On the other hand, camping in the immediate future was out of the question, with tent and sleeping bag unserviceable. I had planned to cut inland and head for the north coast after Golspie, but that route would take me across what is probably the most remote wilderness in Britain. My best hope for a bed that night would be to stick with the east coast and head for Helmsdale, where I knew there to be a youth hostel, and I made up my mind to try that. The change of plan continued the pattern which had started back on 'day one' and, in a sense, I was unperturbed, for one way was no better known than another... and it was an adventure by whichever route.

"Let's go into town now and telephone. We may be able to get something to eat!" I said, suggestively ... but David groaned and asked instead:

"Can I stay here?"

The platform was still deserted and I couldn't see the harm in it, so I left David and the bags and went ahead into the high street. One or two people were out and about, either with dogs or heading for the paper shop, which had just opened. I bought some chocolate and made the call, telling myself that farmers are always up early but, even so, I apologised for phoning at an ungodly hour. Mrs Ritchie, the

CHAPTER 17: THE MORANGIE FOREST – GOLSPIE

farmer's wife, sounded bright and breezy. I was told it was "ne bother" and not to be worrying myself: "…The wee laddie will be just fine."

I returned to the station to break the news, and the chocolate. By the time I got there, someone else had arrived, which I took to be a good sign. Anyone who has regularly commuted by train knows that you can come onto a crowded platform and tell that the train is due and conversely that an empty platform may mean that you've missed it! Sure enough, others arrived and so, after a while, did the train.

I watched as the boy's carriage rolled away and I stood for a moment on the once more deserted platform. In total, David had walked around seventeen miles and I supposed that the experience must have been memorable for him, if not for entirely the best of reasons. I had enjoyed his company, but being alone again now didn't seem strange, it felt normal. Barring further calamity, less than four days' walking now separated me from the finish, the remaining distance being about the same as from London to Portsmouth. I knew that my legs ought to be up to the challenge, even if my kit wasn't and, in spite of the problems so posed, my confidence was high. If you had seen me, that morning, passing back through Golspie, you would have seen a big smile on my face.

CHAPTER 18

Golspie – Lybster

IN WHICH
...with sun, sea, sand and castles, my luck takes a turn for the better, as I make my mark in crofting country

There are no coves or caves and no towering cliffs along that stretch of the coast. A string of footpaths took me from the town over fields of halophytic grasses with clumps of yellow gorse along a flat strip of land. To the left, mounds of rock rose at a gentle angle, and to my right there was a strip of sandy shale and the sea itself, which was air force blue and almost totally calm. I threw some stones into the water, and then remembered that those beaches are frequented by seals. I had no desire to be the gratuitous author of a freak accident, nor to be reported to the RSPCA,[55] and so returned to the arguably less mindless business of walking from one end of Britain to the other!

Against the skyline there came into view the pointed white turrets of Dunrobin Castle, mighty ancestral seat of the Dukes and Earls of Sutherland since the 13th century (although large parts of the four-storey construction are much later additions). On the approach, I came across small groups of oriental photographers who, I presumed, in search of a panoramic shot, had strayed from their main party. One man even photographed me. Typical Scotsman returning from haggis hunt?

I joined the throng and had a quick stroll around the castle's meticulously kept formal gardens before beating a retreat to the coastal

---

[55] The Society for the Prevention of Cruelty to Animals was founded in 1824. Sixteen years later, Queen Victoria granted the society its royal status and so it became the Royal Society for the Prevention of Cruelty to Animals.

CHAPTER 18: GOLSPIE – LYBSTER

track and solitary contentment. The path took me directly into Brora, a bustling town and lively holiday resort popular for fishing and golf. I stocked up in the supermarket, had an early lunch and wrote some postcards.

"Dear girls, In spite of getting wet I should make it to John o' Groats on Sunday around 1.00 pm. See you there! Love from Daddy"

As the cards went into the box I said to myself:

"Now I *have* to do it."

To the north of the little harbour at Brora are the golf links and a beautiful sandy beach which would be perfect for beach cricket, in the unlikely event that you could raise a side in those parts. The tide, by this time, was out. I had the beach completely to myself and, having walked over a mile across virgin sand, stopped to photograph my footsteps trailing back into the distance. As far as I could see, the single track, left right, left right, marked the sand. It seemed to epitomise everything I had done during those weeks. I found myself, on that beach, in the binary opposite of commuter hell when leaves on the track mean "service cancelled", or when signs go up giving the message: "Major roadworks ahead. Expect delays for 14 weeks." It was one of those 'hot moments' when scales fell from the eyes. I was suddenly seeing parallels and glimpsing 'The Big Picture': we tread our path through life. Sometimes we make our mark but (unless you happen to be a Neil Armstrong,[56] and somehow make long-lasting footprints) soon enough we are gone and forgotten. "Time and tide wait for no man", I mused, reckoning that my prints would stay there for a while yet, at least until the tide turned ...and I noticed, from the impressions left, that there were still some areas of good tread left on my boots. Perhaps it wasn't quite all over yet!

---

[56] Neil Alden Armstrong (1930-2012) went on an expedition, in 1985, to the North Pole with Edmund Hillary, the conqueror of Mt. Everest. Armstrong said he wanted to see the North Pole at ground level, because he had only ever seen it from the moon.

Beyond the links, I rejoined the grassy coastal path. Nestling there was a golf ball, not so unusual in itself, but its location intrigued me. I am no golfer but I estimated that this ball had cleared what I took to be the ninth green 'by a mile', metaphorically speaking. This was no near miss. The footballing equivalent would be, perhaps in one of those tense penalty shoot-outs (at which our national team habitually snatch defeat from the jaws of victory) if the striker stepped up and blasted the ball not only over the bar, but over the stand and out of the ground as well. I stooped to pick up the ball, and examined the marking:

"HI DISTANCE", it read, which tickled me, not only because it had clearly lived up to its name but also because it struck a chord with what I was doing. Superstitious? Not I. The ball was not any omen or lucky charm, but it was a pleasing find and I kept it with me to the very end.

People say, "What goes around comes around". I have never been entirely sure about its precise meaning but, if with the flood, Lady Luck had run out on me, that afternoon she returned to my side, in the form of hot sunshine and a strong and gusty, warm, onshore breeze – perfect drying conditions!

Rather like a newly-weds' getaway car, I was already trailing various bits and pieces, footwear and the like, dangling from the rucksack, blowing in the wind. I now made another impersonation, by completely unfurling my purple and black soggy sleeping bag and attaching it to the top of the pack, so that it billowed behind me like a superhero's cape. So attired, I walked all afternoon, at first along the narrow coastal plain and then, when that was no longer possible, beside the A9, all the way to Strath Ullie and the town of Helmsdale.

The most striking features of Helmsdale are the handsome buildings which line the river of the same name, and its two bridges. Through traffic is now carried by a modern structure, functional and very high, at the mouth of the river. The elegant old bridge, just

CHAPTER 18: GOLSPIE – LYBSTER

A quiet coastline and the track north.

Duncansby Head.

upstream, is by Telford and altogether more attractive. From there I contemplated a second bridge jump, but decided against. In the bar of the Bridge Hotel the locals agreed that such a stunt would be madness, although someone reckoned it would be possible to leap from the new bridge at high tide... All the same, that man said he wouldn't try it himself!

The youth hostel did indeed provide me with a warm, dry bed for the night and I was able to march out in the morning well rested and reorganised. My sleeping bag needed more of the Superman treatment, but the rest of my equipment, like my roll-up mattress and the rucksack, had dried pretty well. I hoped that the sticky tape repair to the cracked support rod of my tent would hold up, as I knew that if anything were to go wrong in the wilderness ahead of me, I could be left isolated and exposed.

Beyond Helmsdale, there is no longer a coastal plain, so the railway is forced to follow a broadly westward route inland up the strath, but the road snakes a winding path up into the heather-clad hills above steep cliffs and the sea. Snow poles define the route and there is provision to close the main road completely in winter conditions. Grateful not to be in a blizzard, I walked briskly beside the road, working on the words of my ballad, which was also nearing completion. I thought about the children back at school and hatched the idea of performing the song, with them, possibly during an assembly, to which I could invite someone to receive the sponsorship money. I had the tune and the harmony already in my head. It would be an easy matter to make a musical arrangement for the instruments the children were learning ...but I was struggling with the words! Parts of final verse were coming together:

CHAPTER 18: GOLSPIE – LYBSTER

"His boots had worn out thin, me boys
and his feet were red and raw
Yes, his boots had worn out thin
and his feet were mighty sore
He cried: "If ever I get to John o' Groats
I'll never walk ne more!"

Slave to the physical geography, at the settlement of Berriedale the road plunges dramatically almost to sea level where there is a valley and a confluence of two little rivers. Traffic virtually grinds to a halt at the sharpest of bends by the narrow crossing and then crawls up the other side not much faster than I was walking. At Dunbeath there is another castle, perched on the cliff edge, and a shop. I was sold bread and some expensive cheese, which I consumed immediately, on the hoof.

Before long and to my relief, I came to an inn, The Inver Arms. It was empty inside. Blankets had been laid out over the carpets and upturned chairs were piled up on tables at the side of the room. I assumed the establishment to be closed for redecoration and had turned to go out, when a lady popped up from what seemed to be a hiding place under the bar, apologising for the chaos and asking what she could get me.

"I see you're going to repaint," I ventured.

"Oh no!" she replied. "It's the sheep."

I was very confused, but sensing as much, the woman explained that they were preparing for a sheep market-cum-festival, and hence the blankets. The bizarre image of a lounge bar full of prize sheep was still too much and I spluttered across the foamy head of my pint. Now it was my turn to apologise:

"Excuse me?"

Looking me in the eye, from across the hatch, she was motionless for a moment, then her expression changed as she realised how firmly I had grasped the wrong end of the stick. Sympathetically, she continued to explain:

"No, the sheep will be outside in the yard. We don't want dirty boots spoiling the carpets."

"I thought you meant the sheep came in here.... but I suppose they're *baa*-rred!"

She groaned at my terrible joke and then left me to get on with her work ... or perhaps to escape. Before I left the pub, the landlady did come back, asking me about what I was doing and contributing sponsorship.

It is just possible to see across the Moray Firth from there. For a moment I wondered if it was Scandinavia or Iceland in the distance, because the north coast of Aberdeenshire certainly seemed like another country. No wonder, for a quick check on the map confirmed that I was looking at country twice as distant as Calais is from Dover. Not trusting my mathematics any more than my geography, I decided against trying to calculate such things as the curvature of the earth, and instead told myself just to enjoy the view, blue skies, sunshine, sparkling sea and the faint outline of mysterious grey mountains beyond.

There is a very interesting museum of crofting life near Latheron, where I made my next pit stop. I had seen some evidence of the slender, demarcated plots of land which, together with the dwelling places erected within, constituted crofts, but I had no idea of the pressures and hardships endured by the crofters themselves. Part of the problem was that following Culloden in 1746 and the Disarming Act (which prohibited the wearing of Highland dress, playing the bagpipes, speaking Gaelic and so forth), social conditions deteriorated. The landlords, owing fortunes to the Crown, hammered their tenants and, eventually, once those unfortunate farmers had been squeezed out, land was rented instead to English sheep farmers.

Things had never been all that comfortable for the crofters. The prime plots were taken by family or friends of the landlords; they

CHAPTER 18: GOLSPIE – LYBSTER

in turn sublet smallholdings to local people. Since it was so hard to eke out a living from these steep or stony plots, many crofters were forced to supplement their livelihoods with fishing or producing kelp. Kelp is the ash, rich in potash and of value to glass and soap industries, produced when seaweed is burnt. There was plenty of seaweed in those parts (I had wrestled with fistfuls in Loch Fleet when I was trying to retrieve my camping equipment) and especially on the Atlantic Coast …but the whole kelp industry collapsed in the early 1800s, when potassium-rich mineral deposits discovered on the continent provided a cheaper and more accessible alternative, driving another nail into the coffin of a passing crofting life.

In the museum I met and received more sponsorship, from some Yorkshire ladies who were touring the Highlands by coach. They were from Huddersfield and were pleased to hear how I had been through their home town. Perhaps not surprisingly, they knew Holmfirth very well, but they did not know The Red Lion at Lockwood, or the kindly Mr Kelly who had taken me in.

With the sun over my shoulder and the sea to the side, I continued for several miles along the road, feeling fine, and then at Lybster, the unmistakable sound of bagpipes caught my attention. It was coming from outside the Portland Arms Hotel, where another coach party, visitors this time from America, were disembarking, to be put through a complete 'Scottish experience'. It seemed to make sense to get to the bar before the tourists, so I did. The piper piped on, surrounded and photographed, then led them inside to what became a pre-traditional Scottish tea sing-song, with requests and beer. We had 'The Skye Boat Song', 'O Flower of Scotland' and 'Scotland the Brave' (rather better played than I managed in Inverness) before someone asked:

"Do you know 'Danny Boy'?" and after that:

"'I Left My Heart in San Francisco'."

I was probably raising a wry eyebrow when spotted by their tour guide, smartly dressed in company colours. She stood beside me at the bar and was saying things like:

"Yes, I know ..." And: "So long as they're enjoying themselves," when someone banged the bar and announced in style reminiscent of pompous MCs at wedding receptions:

"Ladies and gentlemen, your Scottish tea is served!"

"Aren't you going with them?" I asked the guide, as the room emptied.

"Not likely!"

While the tour party, presumably, tucked into Scottish scones with Scottish cream and Scottish jam, we were left to exchange names and stories. Jill was from Brighton and her driving ambition was to see the world.

"You've seen quite a bit of Britain, though," I observed, very conscious of where we were, but her sights were set wider still, having plans to cycle across Africa. She was raising sponsorship money herself for the trip. It was obvious to me that Jill had brought many such tour parties to that hotel, she knew her way around the premises, and the schedule was routine.

"They will be happy for at least an hour," she assured, with an air of mischief. "Don't go anywhere." She stood up, stroked my cheek and chin with the back of her hand and disappeared, glancing over her shoulder as she did so. I did as I was told, and waited, coolly sipping my drink, wondering what would happen next.

Beaming, she returned, not alone but with a selection of her party whom she had extracted from the scone-eat, to effect introductions and offer them the chance of lightening their wads of British banknotes by sponsoring me. As they were doing so, from behind their backs, their guide winked at me and gave me the hand signal which scuba-divers use, meaning "Okay".

Everybody wished everybody good luck and I left Jill to gather up her party. I think they said they were going to a castle for a Highland supper. Surely haggis was on the menu!

CHAPTER 19

Lybster – John o' Groats

IN WHICH
…I meet a mass murderer, escape a 4000-year-old curse, learn about 'The Flow Country' and finally receive a welcome at the end of the road.

I decided to look for somewhere to camp and was heading down a side road back towards the coast, enjoying the sunset, when I caught up with an old boy, walking bolt upright, and his whippet.

"Good evening."

"Good evening to ye."

He turned head and shoulders stiffly towards me and smiled through yellow and black teeth, not dissimilar, I recalled, from those belonging to the old cider farmer I had met on the Somerset Levels. With the old dog trotting along beside his master, we continued together along the lane. Quite why he told me, I am not sure – but he had hurt his back as a young man in the days when he would go out with a flashlight and a club, to collect rabbits. (I guess that nightclubbing means something different these days, although it seems to me a shame on our testosterone-pumped night-lifers that their nights out do sometimes also end bloodily.) He used, so he told me, to carry a huge sack, into which he could put forty brained rabbits.

"How many rabbits do you think I could fit into my rucksack?" I asked.

For a moment the old man said nothing, as if calculating; then he stopped in his tracks. The dog stopped and so did I. He looked at me, and the rucksack, and then:

"Fifty rabbits," came the measured reply. It seemed funny at the time and still tickles me, not only by the manner of delivery and how he specified the units, but also by the notion of it. Perhaps there was a new angle for the 'admen' to explore: "To all you mass-murdering rabbit slayers out there... Buy our ergonomically designed super-duper jumbo rucksack and increase your takings by up to 22.5%."

In the end, I camped a little to the north of the village, beside the road which would take me inland, across country, to the north coast and the final miles to the finish.

With less than thirty miles to go, my last full day of walking began as many others had begun over those weeks, with the ritual of sorting out and packing up; although on this occasion, no great time was spent on route planning. The lane was flat and almost dead straight. There were one or two buildings and, I think, one car which passed, in about three hours of walking. The lasting image is of deserted, flat and boggy land on either side of the road, with clumps of heather and narrow drainage ditches full of dark orange water.

Sometimes referred to as 'the Lowlands beyond the Highlands', that area of Caithness forms part of the largest area of blanket bog in Europe, spreading in a band across the far north into Sutherland. In spite of the drainage, which apparently has improved the quality of farming land, there were surprisingly few animals about. Ponies on Dartmoor, sheep high up in the Pennines, and the deer on the Cairngorm Mountains had been a presence even in the wildest and sparsely inhabited areas I had crossed. Here, in the 'Flow', as it is known, there is a difference. The land is beautiful in its way, for its emptiness and calm, but it is also utterly desolate. Nobody would hear your shout, nor would you be likely to disturb anything from its order, save perhaps for the odd small bird or rabbit whose ancestors escaped the club at least long enough to have become parents.

I stopped to investigate a historic archaeological site of some significance known as the Grey Cairns of Camster. From a distance, they looked like giant grazing woodlice, their stone exoskeleton

CHAPTER 19: LYBSTER – JOHN O' GROATS

encasing burial chambers, fully four thousand years old. The National Trust for Scotland/Scottish Heritage have opened up and restored one of the cairns to its original condition, and it was by the entrance to this that, whilst eating a packet of biscuits, I was swarmed by midges. It was the only time that this happened to me on such a scale and left me wondering if the attack was part of some ancient curse. I thrashed wildly about, clapping and swatting, at the same time as reaching for my waterproof. They went for my bare legs, hands and wrists and the small oval around my nose and eyes, which was left exposed after my cagoule was zipped up and the hood pulled tight. I ran away, manfully, pursued by midges, who eventually lost interest, I can only assume when each and every one was sated, with a bellyful of my blood on-board. Midges really can be murder.

The lane continued its direct route for a few more miles, which I trod in trance-like state of reflection and contemplation but, by a slight incline, my attention was caught by some farm buildings, known as Badlipster, and the sounds of human activity. I was no longer alone. Someone had come out into the yard. I waved and called 'hello' and the person waved back. I thought little more of it, but a few minutes later I heard a car coming up behind me. The road, like most in that area, was single track, with passing places. By that stage, I had a pretty fair idea about the different way people drive cars in various regions and in particular how drivers pass pedestrians on the road. It may be wrong to generalise, but it seemed to me that muddy Land Rovers in rural regions are more likely to give you time and space, while shiny saloons on day trips out of town are more likely to make you dive for the ditch! By contrast, this driver was extremely considerate, following me, at my walking pace, for at least a minute, until we came to the next passing place. She waved and drove on, clearly in no hurry. About ten minutes later, I saw her car returning. A little ahead of me, she stopped the car and approached on foot. She was waving an envelope, for me, on which was written one word: 'Hello'.

"Hello," I read out loud, in reply.

"Hello!" she repeated. "Open it."

And so I did. Inside was a card and a greeting which welcomed me to Caithness. She had added: "May your journey be full of magic". I confess to feeling somewhat disarmed by her approach, which seemed about as direct as the road at that point and again I thought that people don't do things like that where I live. She wore jeans and purple nail varnish, to match her top, and spoke in a soft, musical voice:

"Would you like a lift?"

Not since the Tamar crossing at Gunnislake had someone asked me that. I didn't want to accept one then, nor did I now, not least because she appeared to be heading back towards Badlipster, in the opposite direction to where I wanted to go. But she didn't seem in a hurry, so we talked by the roadside for some time. One thing was clear, that she dearly loved the country in which she lived and worked, as a Flow Country development officer. By chance, I had come across the ideal person to tell me about the area, which she was happy to do. In all the time we spent there, no other vehicles came so her car stayed exactly where it was, blocking the road.

The card must have come from Watten, a small village by the edge of a loch with a road junction, a shop, telephone box and a pub, The Brown Trout Hotel, which, you may guess, was to be my next stop. In the small front room a handful of locals and fishermen were in earnest debate over the proposed devolution issue, taxes and the reliance of their community upon the motor car. I did no more than listen, for it was interesting to note that although, to these good people, government in Westminster seemed a long way off (about seven hundred miles), in truth, a government in Edinburgh, centred in that populous belt at the other end of their country, didn't promise to represent their needs any better. Whatever the ins and outs of the arguments, I could quite see that to exist in those parts without a motor vehicle would be very tough. There were places I had passed

CHAPTER 19: LYBSTER – JOHN O' GROATS

from where a trip to the local store might take you all morning and, even with a car, to go to the supermarket via the bank, Boots and 'Woolies' could be a round trip upwards of a hundred miles, well beyond walking distance, in the normal run of affairs.

The railway link between the towns of Thurso and Wick passes besides Loch Watten. I crossed the tracks and found my way to another long, straight and virtually unused lane, which took me to a point about nine miles from the comforts of The Brown Trout.

The landscape there is featureless to the extent that I had lapsed into the mentality of a sheep-counting insomniac: there were no sheep to count, but I did the next best thing, which was to count the telegraph poles as I passed them by the roadside! I suppose I must have reached a hundred, several times over, when a slight tightening in my calf muscles alerted me to the fact that I was walking uphill. So what? Well, as I crested the incline, I realised that a view of the north coast was opening up. Patchy grass and heather to either side swept gently down to the shoreline. The island of Stroma was clearly visible, a slim, grassy pancake separated from the mainland by a slither of silvery grey, and much further out, Hoy's mountainous outline, as well as other of Orkney's isles in the distance. It was a moving moment, which I made the most of by stopping right there and, sitting on my rucksack, watching and waiting for the sunset.

The drop in temperature galvanised me into action. Although the youth hostel at Canisbay was within reach, I decided to camp just where I was. Somehow, to sleep under the stars seemed right.

I hardly slept a wink that night. Excitement and a tremendous sense of expectation were certainly factors, but the main reason for my restlessness was bitter cold. Given the time of year (after all, it was still August) I did not expect a ground frost… but there was one! Even wearing all the clothes I had and cocooned in my lightweight summer sleeping bag, I couldn't get warm enough to rest properly. Instead, I did as I had done under the starry skies near Haworth and turned around and lay on my back with my top half out of the tent. It was a still night and crystal-clear. The brightness of the stars positively invited contemplation about the vastness and beauty of creation.

I have never been to the desert and seen the stars at night, but I would guess that what I was looking at, that night, was no less spectacular. I watched the moon cross the sky and then, in the twilight, surges of electrical activity in the atmosphere made faint arcs of light on the horizon, anticipating the dawn.

The sunrise itself was terrific. Swift and powerful, our star appeared red only for a moment before sending dazzling streaks of gold yellow in a flood across the land. I packed up for the final time and rejoined the road, grateful to feel once more the sun's warmth. By now the waters of the Pentland Firth were deep blue. In the morning light, Stroma was a good deal clearer. I could see a little beach which would be perfect for landing a rowing boat, I imagined, or for sunbathing, especially if you happened to be a seal!

I passed the youth hostel, where the warden and his friend were sitting outside enjoying steaming coffee in the sunshine. I was feeling peckish and asked if he had a store. A packet of fruit digestives or a tin of tuna would have gone down well!

"Sorry," he answered, "you'll have to go on to Groats. It's three miles."

I went down to the shore, and threw some stones into the sea, having checked for aquatic mammals. In fact, I had several hours to kill. My wife would have a gruelling one hundred and thirty-mile drive up from Beauly along the winding A9, so I took my time strolling eastwards, over the beaches, towards my destination.

The tide was quite high, and at one rather slippery rocky section, I decided to cut back inland, not really wishing to fall at the last, or end up with a twisted ankle. Having negotiated the Lairig Ghru, and dismounted Hadrian's Wall without breaking anything other than sweat, it seemed prudent to plump for the grassy fields.

CHAPTER 19: LYBSTER – JOHN O' GROATS

Following tyre tracks through a gap between slate fences, I came out on the coast road by a farmhouse. The farmer himself was standing by the gate leading out of his property. At least this farmer didn't have a gun!

"Lovely morning, isn't it?" I ventured, with a degree of optimistic nonchalance.

"Aye," he said, for it was undeniable and, what's more, he didn't seem to be remotely concerned about my trespass. Instead, he asked where I was from, so I told him, and added that I thought he was lucky to live where he did. I told him how people queued every day in traffic on the M25... and he said that he wouldn't like that.

"I don't suppose you have many traffic jams just here?"

"Never," he replied, and then corrected himself. "There was one once... when the tall ships race came here. All the roads were blocked."

As I stepped past him onto the empty road, it was evident that there would be no tall ships race that day, although I did see and photograph the little ferry chugging across from Orkney. It is said that the ferry, in the 15th century, was operated by a Dutchman, Jan de Groot and that the fee was fourpence, an amount which later became known as a groat. There was once an octagonal house for Jan de Groot's eight descendants and joint owners of the estate, an echo of which is the octagonal tower of the John o' Groats House Hotel, built in Victorian times. Once in view, across the flat farmland, I walked the final mile in a state of calm contemplation. I came to a notice which gives tourists (and 'end to enders'):

A WELCOME AT THE END OF THE ROAD

The sign, too, was octagonal. From there, the harbour, the hotel and the cluster of buildings for souvenirs and ice creams, as well as the customisable fingerboard and photographer's hut, are only a minute or two down the road, which leads to the car park and a caravan park. I slipped anonymously into the information centre to buy a fistful of postcards and, purposely avoiding the Start/Finish line painted on the tarmac outside the hotel, I immediately left.

Close examination of a map of that area will reveal that John o' Groats is not quite the furthest corner of the British mainland, which lies another two miles east, along the coast, at Duncansby Head. I took the postcards up to that point. Below the lighthouse, I made for the furthest corner of grassy cliff, took off my rucksack and sat down, cross-legged. On the other side of a low barbed-wire fence, there was another metre or two of land, and that was it. At the start of my journey, I had climbed out on the rocks as far as it was safe to do so; here it was not difficult to decide that enough was enough, besides which, the idea of being squirted with rank fish oil by a displaced fulmar hardly appealed. So I stayed my side of the fence, writing postcards to my friends, sponsors and the people I had met en route.

If ever you go into a pub and see a dog-eared old postcard of John o' Groats, pinned up amongst others, from regulars on holiday in Ibiza, Corfu or Bondi Beach, I suppose that there is a fair chance it will have my scrawled writing on its reverse, because I wrote over a hundred, relaxing there in the sunshine. I described the blue sky and clear blue sea, the ragged cliffs and the outlying islands, but I do not believe I once wrote "wish you were here". It was a private and very pleasant moment, the act of writing the cards refreshing fond memories of people and places. I was not entirely alone, however. In the time I sat there, several people came and went, including a German gent, who wanted to hire a plane, and a family from Berkshire, who became my last sponsors.

Leaving myself just enough time to return to John o' Groats, for the agreed rendezvous, I stood up stiffly, and then bounded back along the track until the octagonal tower once more took on its homing-beacon role. Later, I would pen a few lines and sign my name in the End to End visitors' book (which is housed in the hotel bar)

CHAPTER 19: LYBSTER – JOHN O' GROATS

to complete my membership of the Land's End and John o' Groats Association but, for now, I waited outside.

It wasn't long before my family arrived. With them was the boy, David, looking a good deal drier than when I had last seen him, and his family. There were handshakes, hugs and kisses after which I finally marched over the finishing line, with a daughter in each arm.

The end.

THE THIRTY-NINE MILLION STEPS

End to End Ballad

Jonathan Richards

At a walking pace

SOLO: 'Tis of a fine young tea-cher lad, the sto-ry I will

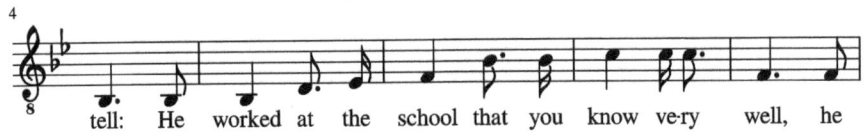
tell: He worked at the school that you know ve-ry well, he

worked at the school, me boys, to earn his dai-ly bread, 'till

CHORUS

one day he said he would try out some-thing else in-stead. He

said, he said, he said, me boys___ one day he said

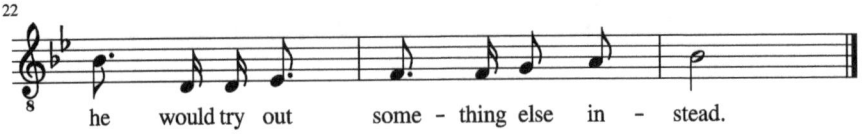
he would try out some - thing else in - stead.

230

THE END TO END BALLAD

The End to End Ballad

(The End to End Ballad was performed in a school assembly, with a folk band accompaniment and the backing support of the children in my class.)

1. 'Tis of a fine young teacher lad the story I will tell
   He worked at the school that you know very well
   He worked at the school, me boys, to earn his daily bread,
   'Til one day he said he would try out something else instead.

All He said, he said, he said me boys.
   He said one day he would try out something else instead!

2. He gathered up some stuff of his and he found his old rucksack
   He loaded up some food and drink and he slung it upon his back.
   He heaved it up on his back, me boys, and set off on a trip;
   He went out a-walking, from England's very tip!

All A trip, a trip, a trip, me boys
   He went out a-walking, from England's very tip!

3. He hadn't been a-walking for all that very long
   When he sat down beside the road with something very wrong:
   There was blisters on his feet, me boys, and pain in his back,
   'Cause he'd packed too much cider inside his rucksack!

All The sack! The sack! The sack for him!
   There was too much cider inside his rucksack!

THE THIRTY-NINE MILLION STEPS

4   That teacher lad unpacked the sack and he had a little think,
He saw what the problem was, so he had a little drink:
"The more that I drink," he thought, "the lighter the load...
and it won't be long before I'll be back out on the road!"

All He drank, and drank, and drank, me boys.
He drank of the cider, to lighten the load!

5   He lifted up the pack again, but the pack was still too heavy,
So he just sat back right down again and he had another bevvy,
He drank the barrel dry, me boys, and tried to find his way,
But had to go and sleep it off down in a field of hay!

All He slept, and slept, and slept, me boys!
He had to go and sleep it off down in a field of hay!

6   Now when the teacher lad woke up the moon was shining bright,
He was feeling in the pink, me boys, and his pack was good and light,
His pack was good and light and so he set back on his way,
And carried on a-walking until the break of day!

All He walked, and walked, and walked me boys.
He carried on a-walking until the break of day!

7   For many a day and many a mile, he carried his pack, 'tis true
And many a tale that he could tell of folk and country, too;
But never was the rucksack full or under so much strain,
For never did the teacher make the same mistake again!

THE END TO END BALLAD

All Oh no, oh no, oh no, me boys!
No never did the teacher make the same mistake again!

8   He carried on a-walking for fully five weeks more.
His boots had worn out thin, me boys and his feet were red and raw
Yes, his boots had worn out thin and his feet were mighty sore,
He cried: "If ever I get to John o' Groats I'll never walk ne more!

All Ne more, ne more ne more, me boys…
If ever I get to John o' Groats, I'll never walk ne more!